"The thief comes only in order to steal and kill and destroy. I came that they may have and enjoy life, and have it in abundance (to the full, till it overflows)." Jesus John 10:10

Enjoy The Good Life

Live Heaven On Earth - The Life God Intended You To Have

SUE INGEBRETSON

authorHOUSE®

AuthorHouse™
1663 Liberty Drive
Bloomington, IN 47403
www.authorhouse.com
Phone: 1-800-839-8640

Published by AuthorHouse 6/20/2013

ISBN: 978-1-4817-6730-9 (sc)
ISBN: 978-1-4817-6729-3 (e)

Library of Congress Control Number: 2013911079

Scripture taken from *The Message*. Copyright © 1993, 1994, 1995, 1996,
2000, 2001, 2002. Used by permission of NavPress Publishing Group.

THE HOLY BIBLE, NEW INTERNATIONAL VERSION®,
NIV® Copyright © 1973, 1978, 1984, 2011 by Biblica, Inc.™
Used by permission. All rights reserved worldwide.

Scripture quotations taken from the Amplified® Bible,
Copyright © 1954, 1958, 1962, 1964, 1965, 1987 by The Lockman Foundation
Used by permission. (www.Lockman.org)

Dedication

I want to give thanks to God the Father and my Lord and Savior, Jesus Christ who has blessed me with every blessing. The Holy Spirit who dwells in me to teach me all I have learned and will continue to learn. I know I have lots more to learn and You are a gentleman in teaching me. I am so thankful that You kept with me and finally got my attention. Having a relationship with my Heavenly Father is the most incredible thing I have ever experienced.

I want to thank countless number of teachers of God's Word. There are many to thank and I know I will meet you in person someday. God has a huge plan for my life and I thank you for being committed to God and teaching the Truth of God's Word.

I want to thank my wonderful husband, Tennis. You have supported me all these years so that I can learn God's Word. What a sacrifice you have made and you will see all God's promises come to pass. I love you dearly.

This book is my gift to my children, grandchildren, family, friends, and to all the people that will read this book. I want you to know the fullness of what you have inherited in Christ so that we can fulfill God's plan for our lives. I want us all to help bring this message of the Gospel to our family, friends, cities, nation, and world. Let's reveal to everyone the real Father, Son, and Holy Spirit.

Table of Contents

Introduction

I wrote this book because I have a great passion to see people receive all that God has for them. Most of my life I believed in God and Jesus Christ but only called on Him when trouble occurred. Over the last few years I have spent much time in the Bible and found out that He is always with me and wants to help me with anything and everything--and I mean He wants to be involved in everything. You see He loves us so much that He sent His Son to die for all so that we could have an abundant life and enjoy it. I learned that God has already provided everything for us in the spiritual realm and all we have to do is believe and receive what He has for us. When we believe, we will receive. Wow--what an awesome deal.

But first you have to believe in your heart and confess with your mouth that Jesus is Lord and that God raised Him from the dead (*Romans 10:9*). You are then saved from eternal punishment in hell. You will spend eternity with Jesus in heaven when you die. But the good news is that eternal life doesn't start when you die, it starts the minute you believe in Jesus Christ (*John 17:3*). No matter what you've done, God wants to have a relationship with you. When you receive Jesus, you are forgiven of your past, present, and future sins. You are made righteous through Christ (*I Corinthians 1:30*).

God wants us to have heaven on earth and be a witness of His amazing love and power on the earth. Jesus Christ was God in the flesh and we are to have a relationship with Father God through Christ through the Holy Spirit and do the same works that Jesus did when He was on the earth. Jesus came to reproduce Himself in us. The devil is the author of sickness, poverty, and oppression of every kind. Jesus came to give us an abundant life. God does not cause calamity and sickness on His children. This is not taught in most churches and we and the people around us are being robbed of what God has for us.

For many years I did not call myself a Christian. The reason for that was because most people that I had come in contact with that called themselves Christians were very hypocritical. They were some of the meanest people I had ever met. So I would just say "I believe in God & Jesus Christ". I didn't even want to claim the name of 'Christian'. But once I got into reading the Bible, I found out what a true Christian was. The term believer is another title for followers of Christ and used as well. The Christians I would run into were very religious. Jesus Christ did not die so that we would have a religion. Religion is man following a bunch of rules and doing good deeds in order to get to God and in order to please Him. Christianity is having a relationship with God through Jesus Christ. Christianity focuses on the heart not outward actions. We don't do good deeds to get God to love us. We want to do good because God loves us unconditionally.

Hosea 4:6 says, *"My people are destroyed for lack of knowledge…"*. That says it all. You can't receive what God has for you if you don't have knowledge of His promises. You can't receive a valuable inheritance from a relative that passed on if you don't know he left you something to inherit. You can't receive something you don't know anything about. I am going to share what I learned about the Bible. I pray that this book will make you hungry for God and dive deep into His Word to find out what He has for you.

Our beautiful United States of America was founded on Christianity. The Pilgrims were actually missionaries that came to the new world to preach the Gospel of Jesus Christ. Why does the United States seem to be drifting away from things that pertain to God? Because we don't have the education that we need--we have been destroyed for a lack of knowledge. The Bible is not taught in school and in my opinion should be the one book that is taught from kindergarten to graduation. There is minimal teaching on the Bible. Many churches are giving a watered down version of the Bible and also teaching wrong doctrine that is short changing what we have inherited through Christ. Many people that claim to believe in God are living like the unsaved people in the world. Most are very rebellious and think they know everything. If I am being positive over a situation that they may think is impossible they say, "That's not reality. I live in the real world." Well, when you are a believer in Jesus Christ, the reality is you live in the Kingdom of God and no longer live in the real world. You will be able to overcome every obstacle that comes your way. God has a way out of everything and He always causes us to triumph. You learn that by renewing your mind to His Word and believing and receiving His promises by faith.

Not only are people rebellious and think they know everything, we have become a nation that is afraid we might step on someone's toes if we stand up for what we believe. The time is now to get back to our Christian heritage and get educated and receive the blessings of God so that we can help someone else. These are perilous times we are living in and it's time to gain knowledge--it's time to get educated and learn what God has for you. He is not the mean God that some people make Him out to be. People get the Old and New Testament mixed up and are living in bondage because of wrong teaching. That is from ignorance which is a lack of education and being unaware of the Truth.

I am here to educate you on the Truth of God's word in a simplified, easy to understand way. No one interprets the Bible one hundred percent correctly and I think it is good to have different ways of looking at some things. But let's make the main things the main things so that people's lives can change. When your life changes, you can impact someone else's life and it just keeps going and going. Are you with me? In this book, I write about the things that changed my life. I write about what we have already inherited as Christians and what we have to do to be effective in the world. Most are trying to get something that they already have but don't know it.

I pray your life will never be the same and that many others lives will be impacted as well. I recommend reading this book several times and seek God. Get into the Word yourself and allow the Holy

Spirit to teach you. You can use this book as a Bible study in a group. Scriptures are listed to back up everything I've written. Get to know your Heavenly Daddy and begin to see how much He loves you and that He has a great plan for you. Don't just gather information--have your own personal relationship with the Father and Jesus Christ through the Holy Spirit. Let me help you get educated and find out what an awesome God we have. You'll be so glad you did.

Chapter 1

God Has Already Provided Everything

The First Thing You Need To Know Is That You Are Loved

I am so glad you are reading this book. God is pleased too because now you can find out what He thinks and says about you. First of all, God loves you more than you can ever understand. I don't know what you have gone through in your life so far, but God knows and sees everything. He formed you in your mother's womb. He says, *"Before I formed you in the womb I knew [and] approved of you [as My chosen instrument], and before you were born I separated and set you apart, consecrating you..." (Jeremiah 1:5 partial).*

You were no accident. Even if you are a child created through rape, you were planned. It doesn't matter what has happened to you or what you have done. You might say, "There is no way God can love a person like me. My parents never loved me". No, God says He approves of you as His chosen instrument. A definition of 'instrument' is somebody used as a means of achieving a desired result or accomplishing a particular purpose. God has a purpose for you. But the first thing you have to know is that you are accepted no matter what has happened. You may have made some bad choices. Well, join the club. We all have. God doesn't approve of us because we are perfect. He approves us because we are made in His image *(Genesis 1:27).*

*"So God created man in His own image, in
the image and likeness of God He created him;
male and female He created them."*

God is real. You cannot see Him but He became a human, flesh and blood person and came to earth as Jesus Christ who lived over 2,000 years ago. *Colossians 1:15* says, *"[Now] He (Jesus) is the exact likeness of the unseen God [the visible representation of the invisible]; He is the Firstborn of all creation."* When you accept Jesus Christ as your Lord and Savior, you now have a relationship with God Who is a Spirit. You will now spend eternity (which starts immediately) with your Father on earth and in heaven. Jesus Christ is the only way to heaven. Jesus said in *John 14:6, "I am the Way and the Truth and the Life; no one comes to the Father except by (through) Me."*

God wants to have a personal relationship with you. You may have heard about Adam and Eve. They were the first humans on the earth that God created. God had created man in His image and they were one spirit. When man disobeyed God, man gave authority to Satan and disconnected from life with God. Man's spirit became connected to the devil. Jesus came to bring us back into a relationship with God the Father. That is why you need to be born again. You are taken from the family of Satan and born again into the family of God. To make a long story short (and you can read the whole story in *Genesis*), they became conscious of what sin was. Before, they didn't even know what sin was. Adam and Eve died spiritually and were separated from their Father and their Father's provision. God still loved them and had already had a plan to get man back to a relationship with God that developed over 4,000 years later. Their sin not only affected them but affected the whole human race. Jesus came to the earth as a Man (God in the flesh) and reconciled us back to a relationship with the Father and His provision.

Satan is a defeated foe and he can't run your life anymore. *First John 3:8(NIV)* states it this way: *"He who does what is sinful is of the devil, because the devil has been sinning from the beginning. **The reason the Son of God appeared was to destroy the devil's work."***

If you are depressed, worried, fearful, hooked on drugs, sick, broke, etc., you can quit following the devil and follow Jesus and have a wonderful life with your Creator who will lead you and guide you. He doesn't care what you've done. When you believe in Jesus Christ, your sins are forgiven, past, present, and future. You no longer have to serve the devil but can lived the good life with God your Father.

God all along has wanted a personal relationship with you and He has a great plan for you. *Jeremiah 29:11* says, *"For I know the thoughts and plans that I have for you, says the Lord, thoughts and plans for welfare and peace and not for evil, to give you hope in your final outcome."* I cover much in this book about what that plan is. Following God is not just for a minister or evangelist. As a kid, I used to think the Bible was only for the preacher to read out of. I had no idea it was written to me so that I could live an abundant, beautiful life. The Bible is your love letter from God and a manual of how to achieve His best so that you can be a blessing to others.

You might say, "I don't want people to think I'm weird". For some reason, religion has made a relationship with God to be something people don't want to talk about. I once was talking to a group of people and I said I could talk about Jesus all day. This guy said, "Please don't". If he only knew. That's my Daddy and I'm in love with Him and He's in love with me.

John 3:16-17(NIV) is the beautiful scripture that you usually hear.

> *"For God so loved the world that He gave His*
> *one and only Son, that whoever believes in Him*
> *shall not perish but have eternal life. For God did*
> *not send His Son into the world to condemn the world,*
> *but to save the world through Him."*

You can see the Father's love for you. He wants to have a relationship with you. A relationship with your Heavenly Father should be the foundation for your life. Eternal life does not start when you get to heaven, it starts the minute you accept Jesus (*John 17:3*). God is so merciful and has provided everything we need to live a blessed life. The only way you will find out what He has provided is to read His Word. We need to renew our mind to what God has said. We need to change from our old way of thinking to His way of thinking. Some of you may be older in age and are pretty set in your ways. There are old religious beliefs that you will have to get rid of. I'll go over things you need to do further in this book. But the foremost thing I want you to know is that it doesn't matter where you are at, what you've done or not done. What matters is that you are reading this book now and can begin a wonderful relationship with your Heavenly Father just as God intended.

Ephesians 2:4-5 says, *"But God-so rich is He in His mercy! Because of and in order to satisfy the great and wonderful and <u>intense love with which He loved us</u>. Even when we were dead (slain) by [our own] shortcomings and trespasses, He made us alive together in fellowship and in union with Christ; [He gave us the very life of Christ Himself, the same new life with which He quickened Him, for] it is <u>by grace (His favor and mercy which you did not deserve</u>) that you are saved (<u>delivered from judgment </u>and made partakers of Christ's salvation)."*

If you are not a believer in Jesus Christ, you can pray the prayer at the end of this book. I recommend you surrender your life to Him. You must ask yourself, "Am I happy running my own life?" You can have the Creator of the Universe run your life. You can follow Jesus and learn from Him. He created this earth and us and don't you think He did an awesome job? Look how intricate our bodies are and how all things were created by Him. It is mind boggling to see all the kinds of animals and bugs, large and small, and each one has a purpose. If God cared about all the animals and bugs and created them for a purpose, how much more does He care about you-His child, created in His image.

David said in *Psalm 23:6, "Surely goodness and mercy shall follow me all the days of my life: and I will dwell in the house of the Lord for ever (KJV)."* When you follow God, goodness and mercy <u>will follow you all the days of your life</u>. You can have a relationship with your Creator and He will direct you and guide you. My life was pretty good but after I made a full commitment to following Jesus, words cannot explain how beautiful my life has become knowing Him and letting Him run my life. Give God a chance. You may not have thought much of Him, but you are always on His mind and He loves you more than words can say!

You must know how valuable you are to God. The first thing Jesus was told by His Father was His identity. *Matthew 3:17* says, *"And behold, a voice from heaven said, This is My Son, My Beloved, in Whom I delight!"* God sees you and me the same way. He is pleased with you. You don't have to perform perfect to be accepted. He loves you just the way you are.

God is portrayed as a mean God, the Man upstairs that is ready to strike you down if you don't do everything right. <u>He is not the God of the Old Testament.</u> When you believe in Jesus Christ, you are redeemed from the curse and now can have a deep, intimate relationship with your Daddy. Religion has not given the Truth of the Old and New Testament. He has always loved us since the beginning. He's not mad at anyone! You are His child and you have an inheritance. He loves you so much. And we love Him because He first loved us (*I John 4:19*).

Being a Powerful Christian

Understanding that God has already provided everything for us is hard to comprehend in our mind. By receiving Jesus Christ as our Lord and Savior, we inherit more than the forgiveness of sins. He has provided prosperity (*II Corinthians 8:9*), healing of our body (*Psalm 103:3 & Matthew 8:17*), deliverance from the oppression of the devil (*Colossians 1:13 & I John 3:8*), forgiveness of our past, present and future sins (*Colossians 1:14*), and eternal life (*John 3:16 & John 17:3*). We don't have to try and get all this, we already have it all in the spiritual realm.

I did not know this. I only thought my sins were forgiven and that I would go to heaven when I died. When I died I would have a mansion in the sky with streets of gold. I never knew He wanted me to have heaven on earth. I thought God was there for emergencies.

But when I found out He had so much more for me, I was elated. I was never told any of this, and maybe someone told me and I didn't hear what was taught. The saddest thing is I never paid attention to the Bible. In my younger years I had never read it for myself. I thought it was only a book for preachers to teach out of. Most of the old religion taught hell and damnation. I thought I had to do everything right and that God would punish me if I made a mistake. I finally heard people teach on the real truth and then did my own investigating.

Something changed in me in October, 2005. I had a huge love for the things of God and got so involved in His Word. I couldn't get enough. Before that, the Bible did not make sense to me. What happened to me on that October day was that I received the baptism in the Holy Spirit. Things started to make sense to me. I look back and now know the difference the baptism made in my life. I am around other people that are Christians and certain things that are in the Bible do not make sense to their mind. That is because they have only been water baptized and not baptized in the Holy Spirit. There is a huge difference. They are trying to make sense of things in the Word through their mind. We cannot understand spiritual things with our mind because they must be spiritually discerned.

> *"The man without the Spirit does not accept the things*
> *that come from the Spirit of God, for they are*
> *foolishness to him, and he cannot understand*
> *them, because they are spiritually discerned."*
> *I Corinthians 2:14 (NIV)*

You can be saved, which means you have acknowledged, confessed and believe in your heart that Jesus Christ is your Savior. You will go to heaven when you die, but that is only the beginning. You will go to heaven if you truly believe in Jesus Christ but will you live a life that will impact someone else on this earth? When you believe in Christ, you are not only saved from hell, you are saved from hell on earth. But there is more to your walk with God than just being saved from hell.

You may think this is a strange way to begin a book, starting with this topic. I put this first because I believe it is the most important truth that most Christians are missing. Don't get me wrong. Most Christians and other religions and denominations love God with all their heart, but they struggle in their daily lives with worry, depression, money problems, and sickness, just to name a few. This is not God's best for His children. When you really think about this, it is quite simple. Sickness and poverty are a curse and we have been redeemed from the curse through Jesus Christ *(Deuteronomy 28 & Galatians 3:13-14)*. Why would God, who is a loving Father, want us sick or poor? You may be a parent and you don't want your kids to be sick. God wants us to live a long life *(Genesis 6:3)*, be prosperous *(II Corinthians 9:8-11)*, and be a witness for Jesus Christ. How can we do that if we are sick and broke? Look up these scriptures for yourself. It's as plain as the nose on your face.

Many have never been taught this and people don't read the Bible for themselves. Many Christians are operating and living as people in the world. There is no difference in their life from the unsaved person in their office. Why? They don't have the knowledge they need and have not received the power source of the Holy Spirit in His entirety.

When we are born again, we receive the Holy Spirit and receive the fruit of the Spirit which changes our character *(Galatians 5:22-23)*. The Spirit of God comes to live on the inside of you. The Holy Spirit baptizes us into Jesus. We are baptized into one body, which is Christ. We are made new creatures and our spirit is made in the image of God. That's where I was most of my life. But yet I had the fruit of the Spirit, I didn't renew my mind to the Word so my fruit was not developing. More on that later. It wasn't until I received the baptism in the Holy Spirit that my life radically changed. This is where the Holy Spirit totally took hold of me--He was in control of my life. I received the full power and presence of God. The Holy Spirit was revealing God's truth to me. When you receive the baptism in the Holy Spirit, the Holy Spirit comes upon you to empower you for service to help others. The power of God will flow out of you. Jesus baptizes you in the Holy Spirit (again-different from water baptism which is an act of faith which demonstrates you going from your old life up into your new life with Christ).

If we take a look at the life of Jesus, you will see that He had no power until He was 30 years old. He was God in the flesh and did not do any miracles until He was baptized and the Holy Spirit descended upon Him in bodily form like a dove (*Luke 3:22*). *Luke 4:1* says: *Then "Jesus, __full of and controlled by the Holy Spirit__, returned from the Jordan and was led in [by] the [Holy] Spirit."* The Amplified Bible says He was full and controlled by the Holy Spirit. The word 'full' means containing as much as possible. The word 'controlled' means to rule or direct influence over. When you receive the baptism in the Holy Spirit, you will contain the full power of God. He will rule and have a direct influence on your life. You will receive power to do what Jesus did when He was on the earth. If Jesus needed the full power of God, we surely do. He was human just like you and me but did no miracles until He received the Holy Spirit. I will talk more about this later.

I can explain this to someone who has been baptized in water and they still don't get it. It is like I'm speaking a foreign language and it is foreign to them because they are not taught this in their church. You can only have faith for what you hear (*Romans 10:17*). Jesus said in *Acts 1:5*: *"For John baptized with water, but not many days from now you shall be baptized with (placed in, introduced into) the Holy Spirit."* Then in verse *8* of *Acts* He says this: *"But you shall receive power (ability, efficiency, and might) when the Holy Spirit has come upon you, and you shall be My witnesses in Jerusalem and all Judea and Samaria and to the ends (the very bounds) of the earth."* They did not receive the Holy Spirit until after Jesus ascended up to heaven. This is the day of Pentecost (*Acts 2*). *Acts 2:4* says, *"And they were all filled (diffused throughout their souls) with the Holy Spirit and began to speak in other (different, foreign) languages (tongues), as the Spirit kept giving them clear and loud expression [in each tongue in appropriate words]."*

You have to be blind not to see the difference. Jesus said that John baptized with water but that the power will come when the

Holy Spirit comes upon you. You will know you have received the baptism by the evidence of speaking in tongues. I will go into this later on as well.

It is hard to understand until this happens to you. To make it plainer, look at the disciples. When they were with Jesus, He told them many things that their mind could not understand.

> *Philip said to Him, "Lord, show us the Father*
> *[cause us to see the Father--that is all we*
> *ask]; then we shall be satisfied".*
> *Jesus replied, "Have I been with all of*
> *you for so long a time, and do*
> *you not recognize and know Me yet, Philip?*
> *Anyone who has seen Me has seen the Father.*
> *How can you say then, show us the Father?"*
> *John 14:8-9*

This did not make sense in their mind. The disciples had been with Him for almost three years and they still could not grasp what Jesus was telling them. He was telling them He was God in the flesh. He was demonstrating the Father on the earth. They were thinking out of their head instead of their heart. They had not yet received the Holy Spirit to be able to discern spiritual things. He was physically present with them and they were looking at Him as human and could not relate to Him in the spirit. Jesus is God in the flesh and He said "If you've seen Me you've seen the Father." They couldn't make sense of this. I believe this is one of the top hindrances to many today. We go by what we see in the physical and leave out the spiritual realm. If the disciples couldn't believe Jesus and He was present with them, how much more do we need the baptism in the Holy Spirit to discern spiritual things today?

You Will Receive Power

Things changed on the day of Pentecost. That is when the Holy Spirit came upon the disciples. They could not receive the Holy Spirit until after Jesus had ascended to heaven. I am repeating this again because of its importance. If you have only been baptized in water and you want more of God, ask Him to fill you to the full with all His power with the evidence of speaking in tongues. You can pray the prayer at the end of this book to receive Jesus Christ as your Lord and Savior and to receive the baptism in the Holy Spirit.

> *"And they were all filled (diffused throughout their souls) with the Holy Spirit and began to speak in other (different, foreign) languages (tongues), as the Spirit kept giving them clear and loud expression [in each tongue in appropriate words]."*
> *Acts 2:4*

> *"But you shall receive power (ability, efficiency, and might) when the Holy Spirit has come upon you, and you shall be My witnesses in Jerusalem and all Judea and Samaria and to the ends (the very bounds) of the earth."*
> *Acts 1:8*

This is when they received power. This power is the Greek word, "dunamis". We get the word "dynamite" from this word.

You say, "I don't get it, I don't see the difference". *Acts 19:2* the Apostle Paul asked some disciples, *"Did you receive the Holy Spirit when you believed [on Jesus as the Christ]? And they said, No, we have not even heard that there is a Holy Spirit?"* So here these disciples were born again and hadn't even heard of the Holy Spirit. Can you see right there that there is a huge difference? The objection that comes up in many churches is that people think that the power that they had back then isn't for today. When you take certain things out of the Bible, you get confused. When you know that we are to do what Jesus did, everything will make sense. But you need the baptism in the Holy Spirit.

When you receive the baptism in the Holy Spirit you will receive all the power that God has for you. You have the same power that raised Christ from the dead (*Romans 8:11 & Ephesians 1:19-20*). This power allows you to have victory in every area of your life and affect other people as well. You will be able to do what Jesus said in *Mark 16:17-18.*

> *"And these attesting signs will accompany those who believe: in My name they will drive out demons; they will speak in new languages; they will pick up serpents; and [even] if they drink anything deadly, it will not hurt them; they will lay their hands on the sick, and they will get well."*

You may say right now, "We can't do that, we can't do what Jesus did. That healing stuff went away with the disciples and I've seen some of those crazy preachers on TV healing people and that stuff is made up." There may be some that aren't following the Gospel completely but you must read this for yourself. We are to do what Jesus did. And also, it's not the preacher's power or our power that these miracles happen. This is the power of the Living God inside of us. Look at what Jesus said in the end of *John 14:10*: *"...but the Father Who lives continually in Me does the (His) works (His own miracles, deeds of power)."* When we are baptized in the Holy Spirit, we have the full power of God to be able to do what *Mark 16* says. We are to even do greater works than Jesus did in His time. Back then there was just Jesus but now He lives in each believer through the Holy Spirit. More and more signs and wonders should be happening.

> *"I assure you, most solemnly I tell you, if anyone steadfastly believes in Me, he will himself be able to do the things that I do; and he will do even greater things than these, because I go to the Father."*
> *John 14:12*

When I read that I was amazed!! We can do the same works that Jesus did, which is laying hands on the sick and casting out demons in His name. This is where some miss the mark. People will only believe parts of the Bible--they pick and choose what they think is true. We are treading on dangerous ground when we do that. The Bible is "the Truth" and the only Truth there is (*John 14:6*). **If you are a Christian and you only believe parts of the Bible you are deceived in a big way**.

If I buy a desk from an office supply store and only take certain parts out of the box to assemble it, it will not fit together properly. It will be weak and not hold up. I need to assemble it the way the instructions say to. I need to use all the pieces. We too must follow God's Word in its entirety and receive all God's power to do what Jesus said in *Mark 16*. Our lives will be powerful and we will be a witness of God's power on the earth for the unsaved people in our lives. People in the church are sick and dying. They are living like people in the world. That is not why Jesus died. His specific instruction to us was to do the same work He did (*Mark 16:17-18, John 17:16-26, John 14:12*).

"Well, what about that stuff about speaking in tongues? That stuff is from the devil." I served the devil for many years and he never once taught me how to speak in tongues. No, this is evidence that you have been baptized in the Holy Spirit. Some may disagree with this but this is what I've found to be true. Read *Acts 2:4* again. I did not speak in tongues when I was first baptized in the Holy Spirit. It took about a year or more and one day some words came out of my mouth. I wrote them down and really didn't do much until one day I was reading a book on the baptism in the Holy Spirit and the Holy Spirit said to me, "Look those words up in Hebrew." I didn't even know any Hebrew but I got in my Concordance and the words I spoke were in there and they all related to water. I was so excited. The enemy was telling me that I was making up those words. But the Holy Spirit revealed to me that I had received the gift of speaking in tongues. I only spoke a few words at first, and months went by and I began to have a whole language that sounded like Portuguese. This gift has changed my life.

Tongues is the Holy Spirit talking to God. You can read more on this wonderful gift in *I Corinthians 14:1-4* as well as in *Acts*. Find a book on the baptism in the Holy Spirit and you will get educated on tongues. To receive the baptism in the Holy Spirit with the gift of speaking in tongues, pray the prayer at the end of this book. You'll be glad you did.

People will still say, "Jesus was the only one who could heal the sick." Read what Jesus said to His disciples in *John 17:20-21(NIV)*.

> *"My prayer is not for them alone. I pray also for those*
> *who will believe in Me through their message, that*
> *all of them may be one, Father, just as You are in*
> *Me and I am in You. May they also be in Us so that*
> *the world may believe that You have sent Me."*

We are all one. Jesus is praying for all that believe in Him. We have authority over sickness just as Jesus and the disciples had. We have the 'dunamis' power of God to speak to our mountains in our lives (*Mark 11:22-24*). Jesus paid the price for our sickness & poverty and defeated the devil over 2,000 years ago. The devil has no authority in a person who is born again. When Christians receive all the power that God has for them by receiving the baptism in the Holy Spirit and learn His Word, there will be a major shift in this world. We will see healthy, wealthy Christians with power helping more and more hurting people know Jesus Christ. Instead, many are barely getting by and letting the enemy run their lives

I come across many Christians who don't know the difference between water baptism and being baptized in the Holy Spirit. Water baptism is an outward symbol of your baptism into the body of Christ. You will receive the Holy Spirit but not in His entirety. Receiving the baptism in the Holy Spirit is receiving all the power of God. You will have the power to lay hands on the sick and cast out demons just as Jesus did. This is done in the authority of His Name.

I know what my life was like when I was without the baptism in the Holy Spirit. I was baptized in water but had not received all that God had for me. Something was missing. I acted like the people in the world. Major change came when I received all of His power. The Word of God became alive to me. The Word of God is spirit and life

(*John 6:63*). The things of God do not make sense to your mind. No one really knows the things of God except the Spirit of God. Your mind is designed to believe what it can see and your spirit is designed to believe the Word of God (what it can't see). Many people do not know this. Most churches do not teach this. But until you experience what I am talking about, you won't know the difference. Christians are not making an impact in the world like God intended. Something is broken.

Jeremiah 2:13 says, *"For My people have committed two evils: they have forsaken Me, the Fountain of living waters, and they have hewn for themselves cisterns, broken cisterns which cannot hold water."* This means that people have forsaken the Holy Spirit. Another word for "forsaken" is to leave behind (Strong's Concordance). Unsaved people are following many kinds of religions and Christians are leaving the full power of God out of their lives. Many are going to church, reading their Bible, and listening to tapes, but still haven't included the Holy Spirit in any of that. They are doing their deeds--which we aren't saved by works (*Ephesians 2:9*)--and not even asking the Holy Spirit to help them understand what they are hearing or reading or asking Him to help them with anything. They are leaving Him behind. That is just a small point of this verse. Some say, "God is always with me". And I say, "But are you always with Him?"

The word 'hewn' means, dig, to cut with blows. That means people are going after something harder than they have to. They are doing things on their own with a lot of effort and not getting anywhere. Christians are going after something they've already got and doing things without the help of the Holy Spirit. They're going to church and reading their Bibles, but when things start to go wrong they panic and their Bible reading that they did without the help of the Holy Spirit did them no bit of good. They are not planting the Word of God in their hearts. The Word of God is seed and has to be planted in our hearts to reap a harvest (*Mark 4:14*). The Word of God planted in our heart has the ability to change our life. Just believing in God isn't going to change you. We have to do some work and get the Word of God in our heart. We have to renew our mind to the Word of God.

The Word of God has to be the foundation for our faith. You can't just pray a prayer and expect God to deliver you out of everything that happens to you. You have to do your part. You have to be connected and the only way you are connected to God is through His Word.

As you saw in *Jeremiah 2:13*, it says, *"...they have hewn for themselves cisterns, broken cisterns which cannot hold water."* If you've got a cistern, which is an artificial reservoir for storing water, and it's not holding any water, it means that something is broken. You've heard the term, "that just won't hold water". If something won't hold water, it is broken and we are operating in a broken system. **We are Christians without the Living Water which is the Holy Spirit**. We are Christians operating on our own instead of depending on the Holy Spirit. God wants us to depend on Him for everything (*John 15:5*). When we do things on our own, we will have minimal results. But when we do things God's way, over and above is all He knows (*Ephesians 3:20*). When we receive the baptism in the Holy Spirit, we will be able to do what God wants us to do with ease. We can be victorious in every area of our lives. We need to receive all the power He has for us, receive His knowledge, and receive all His gifts and give back to others what God has given us. What is happening today is we have Christians without the power of the Holy Spirit and no fruit because they are operating under a broken system. The majority of Christians are operating in their own natural abilities and calling out to God when they have a problem. We are making Him to be like magic. We are not operating spirit to Spirit.

People try to comprehend the Bible with their mind. We need to live disconnected from our mind because the Word of God is spiritual. Jesus said in the end of *John 6:63*, *"...The words (truths) that I have been speaking to you are spirit and life."* He also said in *John 4:24*, *"God is a Spirit (a spiritual Being) and those who worship Him must worship Him in spirit and in truth (reality)."* The bottom line is as humans (natural man), we go by our five senses. God is a Spirit-we cannot see Him. We receive His spirit (when we are born again) and now must communicate with Him through His Word. We are a spirit and we live in a body and possess a soul. If He says that the words that He is speaking to us are spirit and life then the only way we can communicate with God is through renewing our mind to His Word and listening to the Holy Spirit. Remember His Word is spirit and we communicate spirit to Spirit. Walking in the spirit is living a life that lines up with the Word of God. Your thinking must line up with the Word of God and that way will give you life and peace (*Romans 8:6*).

For instance--you are facing a financial difficulty. What a person who doesn't know the Word would say is, "What are we going to do? Do we need to call the bank and see if they will loan us some money? Oh, God, please help us!" But a person who knows the Word and knows their Daddy (yes Father God is our Daddy) says, "Well, it does look bleak but I don't live by what I see. I go by what the Word of God says and I know my Father will provide because the Word says He liberally supplies all of my needs according to His riches and glory in Christ Jesus" (*Philippians 4:19*). In the natural it looks bad but in the spiritual realm God has already provided your need. His Word is spirit and life. Having your supply met is life. Looking at things with your mind is death. Keep focused on Jesus and His Word and He will not let you down. He is faithful.

This is what faith in the Word is. Finding out what God says in His Word and believing Him no matter what things look like in the natural. That is living the supernatural life that God intended. <u>Faith is simple child-like trust in what Jesus has done and faith in His Word</u>. We don't have a faith problem we have a lack of knowledge problem. Jesus said in *Matthew 17:20 "if you have faith as a grain of mustard seed"(KJV)*. If you have mustard seed faith and believe the Word of God and get rid of unbelief, you will see God results. We've all been given the measure of faith *(Romans 12:3)*. We have faith, we just have to release it. We tend to complicate faith when we need to find out what God says and live by it and not by what we see, hear or feel. Christianity has gotten so broken down that most just believe their sins are forgiven and that they are going to heaven when they die. But we need to receive the power of Christ inside of us and start to live the powerful life God wants us to live. We need that to impact the world. We need to start bearing fruit in every area of our lives so that people will take notice of Christians. *Matthew 7:20* says, *"You will fully know them by their fruits."* When people see the fruit our lives are bearing, they will want a personal relationship with our wonderful Jesus. People need to see the signs and miracles of our Mighty Lord and Savior working today (*John 4:48*). When someone hears your testimony of how you have been healed of cancer and that God sent His Word and healed you (*Psalm 107:20*), they would have to be dead not to want to find out more.

Signs And Miracles Will Bring Followers

The world says "I won't believe it until I see it." But in God's system, we believe then we see. God has many gifts and it is a shame when we don't receive all He has for us. He is our Heavenly Father and cares deeply. There are great churches all over but a lot of pastors do not talk about the baptism in the Holy Spirit, the gift of tongues, healing & prosperity. It is in the Bible and all of this is for us today. God wants to show up and show out in these last days and He can't do it with Christians that don't have any power.

There needs to be signs and miracles today. That is the only way people will follow Christianity. If someone is raised from the dead or blind eyes are opened, then people may believe after they see these miracles. Jesus said in *John 4:48, "Unless you see signs and miracles happen, you [people] never will believe (trust, have faith) at all."* If Jesus needed signs and miracles in His day, how much more do we need them?

If you have a book of Mormon beliefs, a Muslim Koran, and a Christian Bible laying on the counter, what is to stop you from believing parts of all three? But if someone is raised from the dead or healed of cancer because they stood on the Words of Jesus Christ and spoke to the mountain (*Mark 11:22-24*), you will believe the Bible of the One True God. The Apostle Paul said in *I Corinthians 2:5, "That your faith should not stand in the wisdom of men, but in the power of God."(KJV)* That is the 'dunamis' power of God which is the mighty power of God to overcome anything that comes against you. It means ability and might. We can't just go to church and sit there thinking we did our duty to God for the week. We need to renew our minds to the Truth of God's Word and do what God predestinated us to do. To predestine is to decide in advance what is going to happen. *Romans 8:29* says, *"For whom He did foreknow, He also did predestinate to be conformed to the image of His Son, that He might be the firstborn among many brethren."(KJV)* We are to be conformed to the image of Jesus which means we are to behave as Him. That is the call of God for <u>everyone</u> who believes in Jesus Christ. Jesus said, *"This is My commandment: that you love one another [just] as I have loved you."* *(John 15:13)* We are to love one another as He loves us and do what He did. We are to cure the sick, raise the dead, and drive out demons, just to name a few *(Matthew 10:7-8)*.

There are many different philosophies about the Word of God. Some are false, some are watered down. Some pastors are only giving a 'feel good' message because they want to draw as many people as they can. They say, "We don't talk about the baptism in the Holy Spirit in church" or "we don't believe those miracles are for today. We don't think that everyone can be healed. God is waiting to heal that person when they get to heaven". What a bunch of hogwash! I am not condemning anyone. People are destroyed for lack of knowledge. Many have theological teaching which has been watered down. We need to pray that these pastors and churches would know the Truth and start to preach it. We can't condemn people for what they don't know. We need to love them. Once signs and wonders are appearing, then people will take note. Let's get educated and do the works of Jesus. This is for everyone--not just for preachers!!

Change Your Way of Thinking

When you are baptized in the Holy Spirit, the Bible will make more sense to you. The Holy Spirit will teach you all things *(John 14:26)*. Of course this takes time so you must renew your mind to the Word of God *(Romans 12:2 & Ephesians 4:23)* **on a daily basis**. We will talk more about this in chapter three. You feed your body food.

If you did not feed your body food you would not have any strength. Our spirits are the same way. We must feed our spirit's the Word of God. His Word is our only connection to His blessings so we need to feed our spirit the Word. You must learn to think like God thinks so you can have what God says you can have.

I hear people say, "I have faith, I believe in Jesus." I ask them "What do you believe? What do you have faith for?" Most don't know how to answer that. Why? Because they haven't read enough of the Word to renew their mind. They don't have the Word of God in their heart. They only have it in their head, if that. They think just because they believe in Jesus Himself that that is their faith. You need to know what you have faith for and find out the will of God and that comes from reading His Word (*Romans 12:1-3*).

I believe the majority of Christians have human faith. Their faith is based on what they can see, feel, and hear. Human faith relies on the five senses. People look to themselves to meet their needs. The faith of Jesus is knowing that God has already done and provided everything for you and you rest in His finished work. God kind of faith stands on the Word. It is the invisible over the visible. An example is Jesus paid the price for our salvation and died knowing He would be raised from the dead. If the Father says it is going to happen then faith says I believe it. If the Word says your needs are met according to His riches and glory in Christ Jesus (*Philippians 4:19*), then believe it. The God kind of faith rests and does not fail. The God kind of faith is committed to what the Word says and believes it no matter what things look like. If we can believe God that we are saved from hell when we believe in Christ, then we should believe Him for everything else. The main problem is people don't know what the Word says and are too lazy to find out for themselves.

We've all been given the same faith Jesus had. The way your faith will increase is by renewing your mind with the Word of God. *Romans 12:2* says this:

> *"Do not be conformed to this world (this age), [fashioned after and adapted to its external, superficial customs],*

but be transformed (changed) by the [entire] **renew**al of
your mind [by its new ideals and its new attitude], so
that you may prove [for yourselves] what is the good and
acceptable and perfect will of God, even the thing which
is good and acceptable and perfect [in His sight for you]."

The Holy Spirit reveals to you the Truth of God's Word and the Truth replaces your old way of thinking. The word 'renew' means to renovate. When you renovate a house, you change the whole inside and outside of it. We are too changed into the likeness of God when we renovate our minds--we tear out all the old way of thinking and replace it with thinking like God. You can only do that by reading God's Word. This is a constant process, especially if we have not been brought up in the Word. We have a lot of work to do to change our old way of thinking. The Word of God must be the main focus of your life if you want to have everything God has for you. The end of *Romans 12:2* says that you will find out what the will of God is for yourself. The will of God is for you to be healed, prosperous, and delivered in every area of your life. The call of God is to be like Jesus. When you change your old way of thinking, you will change your life and be on the path that gets sweeter and sweeter with each passing day. Read and study the Word, listen to tapes and read books on Christianity, and watch Christian television--keep feeding your mind with the Truth.

"But Sue, I go to church every week." You could go to church for 50 years and not change. If I wanted to become a surgeon, I wouldn't become one by going to one class a week. It takes more than that. Renewing your mind is a daily thing. Faith for God's promises will come the more you read and hear the Word. *Romans 10:17 says, "So faith comes by hearing [what is told], and what is heard comes by the preaching [of the message that came from the lips] of Christ (the Messiah Himself)."* It's not that we don't have faith, but faith will increase when you renew your mind. The will of God will be revealed to you so you can affect someone else's life.

By now you are thinking, "That sure sounds like a lot of work. I have a job and I don't know when you expect me to do all this?" How much time you put into the Word depends on how much you want to receive in the Kingdom. We are not **of** this world--we are believers and <u>live in the kingdom of God</u> (*John 17:14 & 16*).

"Well I don't know about you, but I live in the real world. You're not being realistic." I repeat, as Christians we live **in** the world but we are not **of** this world. The reality, as a believer in Christ, is that we live in the Kingdom of God here on earth. Heaven has come down. There is a huge difference. Many people live with one foot in the Kingdom and one foot in the world. They do not live any different than their unsaved neighbor. They will still go to heaven but will not enjoy all that God has for them on earth and not be a very good witness for Christ. You can live a life that is full of joy no matter what happens. Joy is not found in our circumstances but joy is found in Christ alone. Joy is based on our relationship with God not our circumstances. If people are sad, depressed, etc., they are focused on themselves and their circumstances, not God. *Psalm 16:11* says, *"You will show me the path of life; in Your presence is fullness of joy, at Your right hand there are pleasures forevermore."* When you have a relationship with God and find out that Jesus has taken care of everything, you can live heaven on earth but you must renew your mind to this way of thinking. Learning this in the Word is key and not taught in most churches. But you have to make a decision that you want to change and start renewing your mind.

You will need to take a look at your day and see how much time you are devoting to driving in your car or watching TV. If you spend one hour commuting to and from your job, you can be listening to the Word on CD. Are you watching mindless television three hours a night? How about reading the Word or listening to teaching tapes? Devote your time to the Lord instead of watching a trashy movie. You have to ask yourself, do you want to serve the devil or the Lord? And let's not serve both. The choice is yours. You can choose life or death. God even gives us the answer to what we should choose. *Deuteronomy 30:19* says, *"...I have set before you life and death, the blessings and the curses; **therefore choose life**, that you and your descendants may live."*

21

You Are Royalty

When you accept Christ, you are a child of the Most High God. He sees you as royalty. You now rule as a king on the earth and if you see something out of order, you are to put it in order. If sickness comes upon you, you take your authority and cast that out of your body. You carry the power and presence of God in you. *Revelation 5: 10* says:

> *"And You have made them a kingdom (royal*
> *race) and priests to our God, and they shall*
> *reign [as kings] over the earth."*

God sees you just as He does Jesus *(Galatians 4:7)*. *Galatians 4:6* says, *"And because you [really] are [His] sons, God has sent the [Holy] Spirit of His Son into our hearts, crying, Abba (Father)! Father!"* God is our Daddy. God wants us to have a great life so others will want a relationship with Him. You will not be a good witness for Christ if you are complaining and negative. You have received an inheritance "in Christ" and it is **huge**. You have received more than just the forgiveness of your sins. That is major but you have also inherited prosperity, healing of your physical body, and authority over anything that comes your way. But you must read "the will". You cannot receive something you don't know anything about and you cannot receive if you do not believe.

Old Testament Verses New Testament

I hear people say, "that guy really knows the Bible". You must be careful about people like that. Many times those types of people are very religious and look down on others if they have done something wrong. They may know some things in the Bible but do not separate the Old and New Testament.

Many people have trouble understanding the Bible. They will carry the law of the Old Testament into the New Testament-the New Covenant of grace, and will feel condemned about many things and also make you feel bad for doing certain things. You must know that when you follow Christ you are not under the law but under grace and the Father sees us as He sees Jesus. God is not looking at our sin, He is looking at who we are in Christ. *Romans 6:14* says, *"For sin shall not [any longer] exert dominion over you, since now you are not under Law [as slaves], but under grace [as subjects of God's favor and mercy]."* We are righteous and justified because of who Jesus is not based on how we follow rules (*Romans 10:4*).

> *"Christ purchased our freedom [redeeming us] from the curse (doom) of the Law [and its condemnation] by [Himself] becoming a curse for us, for it is written [in the Scriptures], Cursed is everyone who hangs on a tree (is crucified); To the end that through [their receiving] Christ Jesus, the blessing [promised] to Abraham might come upon the Gentiles, so that we through faith might [all] receive [the realization of] the promise of the [Holy] Spirit."*
> *Galatians 3:13-14*

Don't get caught up in all the rules and regulations of the Old Testament where you feel condemned for everything you do wrong or get religious and call everyone a wicked sinner. These are two extremes. Look at *Deuteronomy 28* and you will see blessings and curses. We believers receive the blessings but have been redeemed from the curse. In the Old Testament they were blessed based on their performance. But in the New Covenant (New Birth) we receive all the blessings because of Jesus' performance. He was the perfect sacrifice for us so that we could be free in every area of our lives. This is a beautiful thing when you find out what you have been redeemed from and what you have inherited. You will fall in love with Jesus all over again.

You will be relieved to know that God is not a mean god but a loving Father that has a prosperous life for you in every area. He wants a relationship with you and is not looking at everything you've done or do wrong. When He looks at you He sees Jesus. And Jesus is all together lovely and the Father loves us so much that He sent His Son as the atoning sacrifice for our sins (*I John 4:10*). We find out how Jesus loved and treated people and imitate what He did. The Bible is not just a book of rules or stories for our information. The things that happened are true and happened to people like you and me. The Bible is a book of God's creative power--a love letter and a book of promises and an instruction manual on how to have and live a glorious life. The spoken Word of God has the power to change your life. God spoke the world into existence by His words. Imagine the power you have and don't even know it. We will discuss the power of words in a later chapter.

If you are a new believer, I suggest starting out by reading the New Testament before the Old or read a little of each and see how Jesus is depicted in the Old Testament. That is my personal opinion and doesn't have to be followed. That just worked for me and all those rules didn't confuse me. <u>But as long as you know you have been redeemed from the curse, you should read and start at the beginning</u>. You want to get to know God, your Creator. He made you. You didn't come from a monkey or a piece of slime. And the earth is not billions of years old. It is about 6,000 years old. Don't get me started on that. Dinosaurs existed before the flood and there are scriptures on that in *Job 40* and *41*. The Grand Canyon was created by the flood. Check out these two museums that have evidence of this: Creation Evidence Museum of Glen Rose, Texas and Creation Museum near Petersburg, Kentucky. We have been told a pack of lies about evolution and the Truth has to be told. God has been taken out of most schools and kids are being taught they came from a monkey. I got carried away with that but you need to check out these things for yourself.

The Holy Spirit is your Teacher (*John 14:26*). The Old Testament was a picture of what was to come through Jesus Christ. Christ is depicted in the Old Testament in various instances of a shadow of things to come (*Colossians 2:17*). He was the Passover Lamb whose blood was shed for our sins. His crucifixion happened on the day of preparation for the Passover at the same hour that the lambs were being slaughtered for the Passover meal that evening. That is only one shadow and only God could have planned this out. He's taken care of everything to the very last detail. You've already got everything you need in Christ. His blood was shed and through His blood you are forgiven, healed, prosperous and protected. We now have a better covenant (*Hebrews 9:10*). *Hebrews 9:18* says, *"So even the [old] first covenant (God's will) was not inaugurated and ratified and put in force without the shedding of blood."* Read the book of Hebrews for yourself and see that God through Jesus Christ has made a new and better covenant.

Jesus Christ paid the price for every sin--past, present, and future. Some teach that your past sins are only forgiven and that you need to confess your sins to a priest when you sin again. Jesus is your High Priest *(Hebrews 4:14)*. Jesus died over 2,000 years ago and paid the price for your sins then. He doesn't have to die again so your future sins can be forgiven. Just think about that. There is not punishment and wrath placed upon you because you committed adultery. Jesus paid the price for that. Jesus said in *John 16:8-9, "And when He comes, He will convict and convince the world and bring demonstration to it about sin and about righteousness (uprightness of heart and right standing with God) and about judgment: **About sin, because they do not believe in Me [trust in, rely on, and adhere to Me].**"* The only sin the Holy Spirit will convict you of is not believing in Jesus. If you feel guilty over a sin you've committed, relax. Jesus already paid the price for it. You don't have to suffer again for what He paid for. Your neighbor that believes in Jesus and is a homosexual will not go to hell because of his sin of homosexuality. He would only go to hell if He doesn't believe in Jesus. Of course, that lifestyle is deadly to a person but God loves him or her despite of what they are doing. If you have done something you are ashamed of, repent which means to turn away from. God has forgiven you. Jesus bore your guilt and shame.

God loves us so much He gave His only Son for us. We are the righteousness of God in Christ *(II Corinthians 5:21)*. When we receive Jesus as our Lord and Savior, we don't receive what we deserve, we receive what Jesus deserved. We deserve hell, but instead Jesus paid that price for us and we receive everything He deserves. That is astounding. God sees us as if we never sinned. Some may say that can give a person a license to sin if sin is paid for. No, you won't want to sin because you know how much God loves you.

We are no longer under the Law of the Old Testament but under grace (*Romans 6:14*). Once you know how much God loves you and find out what you have inherited through Christ, you will never be the same. God loves us so much He gave up His only Son for all of us. If He did that, He will give us everything else we need. We don't need to worry but believe.

> *"He who did not withhold or spare [even] His own Son*
> *but gave Him up for us all, <u>will He not also with Him*
> *freely and graciously **give us all [other] things?**</u>"*
> *Romans 8:32*

Our Inheritance

A major revelation I received years ago was that God wants us blessed in every way.

> *"Beloved, I pray that you may prosper in every*
> *way and [that your body] may keep well, even as*
> *[I know] your soul keeps well and prospers."*
> *III John 2*

Another revelation I received was that He had already given me every blessing possible. God's blessing is not something He's going to do--**He's already done everything**. A blessing is not things and stuff, it is an empowerment to prosper in every area of your life. Most Christians are struggling in life trying to get something they already have.

> *"Praise be to the God and Father of our Lord*
> *Jesus Christ, who **has blessed** us in the heavenly*
> *realms with every spiritual blessing in Christ."*
> *Ephesians 1:3 (NIV)*

So why are so many Christians walking around sick and/or afraid of their financial future? "Oh, I don't know what I'm going to do if I lose my job?" They haven't sown the Word of God in their heart. They don't know *Philippians 4:19* which says, *"And my God will liberally supply (fill to the full) your every need according to His riches in glory in Christ Jesus."* If you lose that job, rest and believe God for a better job. Believe His Word. "Oh, but you don't understand. I have a family history of heart disease and with all this stress I know I'll have a heart attack." Why do Christians predict things like this? They're playing God and calling forth their future. Jesus said in *Mark 11:23* that you will have what you say. People don't realize the power of their words. They are not trusting God and they don't know His Word. They don't know they have been redeemed from sickness and poverty. Christians are not suppose to be sick. Look at these two scriptures from Proverbs and Psalms. God has all the answers.

"Trust in the Lord with all your heart and
lean not on your own understanding."
Proverbs 3:5 (NIV)

"Praise the Lord, O my soul, and forget not all His benefits--
*Who forgives all your sins and **heals all your diseases**.."*
Psalm 103:2-3 (NIV)

If people spent time learning the Word and stood on what God says instead of making stuff up in their head or allowing the enemy to put stupid thoughts in their mind, we would see a radical change in the body of Christ. Trust the Word and not your five senses. Trust the Word and not the news report. Quit living out of your mind or the natural world and come on into the supernatural. God's Word is true and He is faithful.

We have been redeemed from the curse (*Galatians 3:13-14*) and sickness and poverty are a curse. "Well, that just doesn't make sense to me. I'm not seeing anything good in my life and I've got a disease where there is no cure. The doctors can't help me. They say there is nothing else they can do". Know that Jesus has been healing longer than doctors. I am not against doctors and there are times you need to go to the doctor. There may be an operation you can have that can save your life. But the first place you should go to is the Word of God. And renew your mind to the truth that Jesus took all your diseases and all your pain on and in His physical body. Don't listen to what the doctors report says, look at what the Word says. Some things in the Word don't make sense to our mind. Again, don't live by how it makes sense to your mind. Live by what the Word says and His Truth trumps what you feel or see. And I repeat, if the doctor says you have clogged arteries and need open heart surgery, believe that God will give the doctor wisdom and guidance and you will recover healthier than before. Bottom line is that God wants you well.

If you're speaking negative (death) over your life, you are allowing your mind to get in the way. Your mind isn't designed to believe God. It's your spirit that believes God. God's Word is spirit and life (*John 6:63*). We have to get our mind renewed with the Word of God so that we live by the Word instead of our five senses. You want what is in your spirit to overtake what's in your soul and body. That is done by renewing the mind (*Romans 12:2*). You must get the Word in your eyes and in your ears then it will get into your heart and become revelation knowledge. Then we speak it out of our mouth and what we say will manifest (*Isaiah 55:11*). Speaking the Word of God out loud brings faith. By believing and speaking the Word, you will have life. A healthy body is life and sickness and poverty is death. Once you know that God has already healed all your diseases, you must stand on **that** Word. As you renew your mind to God's Word and believe it, your soul and body will agree with what you have in your spirit. When sickness comes against you, know that it is from Satan and you can cast that sickness out of your body because it doesn't belong there. You are the same as Jesus and have power over sickness. I'll talk more about this in chapter three.

We don't have to live life defeated. We have received an inheritance. We've received the Blessings of Abraham. Look at what God said to Abram in *Genesis 12:2-3*.

"I will make you into a great nation and I will bless you;
I will make your name great, and you will be a blessing.
I will bless those who bless you, and whoever curses you
*I will curse; **and all peoples on earth** (that's us)*
***will be blessed through you**."* (parentheses mine)

You say, "What are the blessings that I receive?" Read *Deuteronomy 28:1-14*--those are our blessings. We don't receive the curse (*Deuteronomy 28:15-68*) when we make Jesus the Lord of our life--remember, we've been redeemed from the curse through Christ. Anything that is a blessing in the Word is ours. How you ask? Because when you are a Christian you receive "The Blessing" through faith in Christ.

"To the end that through [their receiving] Christ Jesus,
the blessing [promised] to Abraham might come upon the
Gentiles, so that we through faith might [all] receive [the
realization of] the promise of the [Holy] Spirit. 16 Now
the promises (covenants, agreements) were decreed and
made to Abraham and his Seed (his Offspring, his Heir).
He [God] does not say, And to seeds (descendants, heirs),
as if referring to many persons, but, and to your Seed
(your Descendant, your Heir), obviously referring to one
individual, Who is [none other than] Christ (the Messiah)."
Galatians 3:14 & 16

Galatians 3:29 then says, *"And if you belong to Christ [are in Him Who is Abraham's Seed], then **you** are Abraham's offspring and [spiritual] heirs according to promise."*

Let me make it clear to you. If you have accepted Christ as your Lord and Savior then "The Blessing" is yours because Christ is Abraham's Seed and Christ lives in you. We are heirs according to the promise made to Abraham. If you aren't shouting, you are dead!!

How do we receive the Blessing? By faith--not by how good we are but by believing in Jesus! Once you get this deep in your spirit, there is no devil in hell that can stop you from having a life that will be so amazing, everyone will want to know the God you serve. Christ accepts anyone no matter what you may have done or not done. Now, that's good news. That's why the Gospel is called "The Good News". And it is actually called "the too good to be true good news". I sometimes am in amazement on what Christ has done for us and most Christians don't know their full inheritance.

You may say, "I've never heard anything like this before. You mean I don't have to put up with this flu I get every year? You're saying sickness is from the devil and I have authority over it?" Don't trust me, read the scriptures for yourself.

"They don't teach that in my church." Most churches think that Jesus and the disciples were the only ones who could heal people. And it's not us that heal but Christ in us-His power in us. Many churches only teach on the forgiveness of sins. They don't teach you that you have inherited the Blessing (*Galatians 3:13-14, Revelation 5:12*) so that you can live heaven on earth. Where does it say in the Bible that only the disciples and Jesus saw miracles? That doing what Jesus did is not for us today? Show me where it says that! You won't find it. That way of thinking only confuses people. When you know who you are in Christ and what your purpose is, everything will make sense-everything becomes clear. If *Psalm 103:3* says He heals all your diseases, that means **all** your diseases--even the ones the doctor says there is no cure for. If you don't believe God's Word, you are calling God a liar.

I believe many people think some scriptures were only for people in the Old Testament or for the disciples. I'm not quite sure. It goes back to people being destroyed for lack of knowledge (*Hosea 4:6*). Many dispute preachers who teach that we have been healed of all diseases. You are calling God a liar. You are discounting what Jesus did for you. You are cheating others of a blessed life. It is dangerous to pick only what you want to believe. You must read this for yourself. God's Word must be your final authority. Please do not take my word for it. If you don't believe me that you are healed today, then read it for yourself. Jesus fulfilled the prophecy spoken by Isaiah in *Matthew 8:17 (NIV)*, "*This was to fulfill what was spoken through the prophet*

Isaiah: He took up our infirmities and carried our diseases." The King James Version says He bore our sicknesses. Can it get any plainer than that? How do you deny that? Look at the scriptures I've given you and do your own study.

I pray you will see the Truth and begin to live a life that is blessed beyond words. Jesus said in *John 8:31-32(NIV)*, *"If you hold to My teaching, you are really My disciples. Then you will know the truth, and the truth will set you free."* We are actually made free when we know the Truth of God's Word. To 'make' is to transform somebody into something else. And if you are in Christ then you are a new creature-the new has come, you don't become new over time. You are made free from all bondage the minute you receive Jesus as your Lord and Savior. You are not free if you are sick, poor, worried, or depressed. When you know the truth about God's Word, you are made free in every area. You are not immediately set free because you become a Christian and read the Bible one time. That Truth has to become revelation to you and then bondages will be released because you have renewed your mind with what is true in His Word. Some people think this scripture means that if you know the truth about yourself, you will be free. There is some truth to that because if you come clean with things, you may have a feeling of release and feel free. But Jesus is not talking about that. He is saying that when you know the truth about God's Word, you will be free. This takes time. So ask yourself if you are free in every area? If not, I would recommend finding the Truth in God's Word and renew your mind until it become revelation to you. You'll be so glad you did.

We are not just saved from hell, we are to live heaven on earth. *Galatians 1:4* says, *"Who gave Himself for our sins, that He might deliver us from this present evil world, according to the will of God and our Father."* Jesus delivered us from this present evil world which we live in today. We don't have to wait until we get to heaven to be healed and whole. Why would we need that in heaven when we will already have it there? Why would God want us to suffer here before heaven? Do you get that? The blessed life is for us right now! We are equipped to live a prosperous life. You just need to renew your mind and begin to walk it out.

Chapter 2

Love, Give, and Forgive

Love

When I was young, I remember having an attitude of getting even. If someone was mean to me, I would be mean to them. That just seemed like a natural thing to do. Why should someone get away with treating me like they did? It felt so good to get even and hurt someone that hurt me. The revenge usually came through words. I didn't like the physical kind of threat where I would hit someone, but I could sure "slam" them with degrading words. What a way to live. I am so thankful God made me see His way instead of following the enemy's way.

Loving someone who is rude or has hurt you gets easier in your walk with God. You must continue in His Word to get to know God's character. You must renew your mind *(Romans 12:2)*. God is not evil and doesn't get revenge on you if you fail *(Psalm 5:4)*. We need to live for Christ not for ourselves *(II Corinthians 5:15)*. We need to not be concerned on how someone is treating us, but be concerned on how we are treating them.

God's love is not based on what we do or don't do. God's love is based on who Jesus is. God loves us as much as He loves Jesus. When you know that God loves you no matter what you do, you can love others no matter what they do to you. Think about how much God loves you and has had mercy on you. Think about some of the awful and dumb things you may have done and remember how God loved you even when you were doing something terrible. Before you're quick to criticize someone, remember God loving you when you weren't so lovely. It is at that point that it gets easier and easier to love others. *Ephesians 1:4-6(KJV)* says this:

> *"According as He hath chosen us in Him before the foundation of the world, that we should be holy and without blame before Him in love: Having predestinated us unto the adoption of children by Jesus Christ to Himself, according to the good pleasure of His will, to the praise of the glory of His grace, wherein He hath made us accepted in the Beloved."*

> *"Yet now has [Christ, the Messiah] reconciled [you to God] in the body of His flesh through death, in order to present you holy and faultless and irreproachable in His [the Father's] presence."*
> *Colossians 1:22*

Can you see the Father's love for you? It is hard to comprehend that God sees us with no fault. He's not in Heaven looking down at us and criticizing us when we do things wrong. He isn't blaming us for anything. We are accepted because of Jesus. We have to get a hold of how God sees us and know how much He loves us. We are His kids. We need to obey Jesus' commandment in *John 15:12. "This is My commandment: that you love one another [just] as I have loved you."* Once we get a revelation of how much God loves us, then it is the commandment that fulfilled the Law to love one another as Jesus loves us. We have no right to criticize a family member or co-worker that does us wrong. They don't know any better. They do not know how much God loves them because if they did, they would act differently. The call on our lives is to be like Jesus (*Romans 8:29*). We are His representatives on the earth. Our relationship with God has to be number one in our lives. We need to know how much God loves us and learn to love other people. People can't see God, but if we love one another, God abides in us (*I John 4:12*).

When you look at the character of Christ, you see unconditional love, compassion, understanding, forgiveness, and mercy. He was treated horribly by the religious people and He kept a good attitude. I know that He did not like what they were saying to Him or doing to Him, but He loved them so much that He died for them. He said in *John 15:13*, "*No one has greater love [no one has shown stronger affection] than to lay down (give up) his own life for his friends.*" God knows nothing other than love.

"This is love: not that we loved God, but that He loved us and sent His Son as an atoning sacrifice for our sins."
I John 4:10(NIV)

"And so we know and rely on the love God has for us. God is love. Whoever lives in love lives in God, and God in him."
I John 4:16(NIV)

"We love Him, because He first loved us."
I John 4:19

"For God so loved the world that He gave His one and only Son, that whoever believes in Him shall not perish but have eternal life."
John 3:16(NIV)

You may say, "But you don't know what my sister did to me". We should not be concerned on how people are treating us, but should be concerned about how we are treating them. That doesn't mean we let people walk all over us. If this is a challenging thing for you, spend time learning about God's love. Spend time reading about Jesus and how He kept a good attitude when people weren't treating Him right. Love is not an emotion, it is an action. Do you think Jesus felt like going to the cross? If He would have gone on emotion, He would have never finished the work that He was called to do. He went to the cross as an act of love for us. Sometimes you may not feel like loving someone but you can do it. You have a choice to do it or not. *Colossians 3:14* says,

> "And above all these [**put on**] love and enfold
> yourselves with the bond of perfectness [which binds
> everything together completely in ideal harmony]."

The scripture says to "put on love". You may not feel like loving someone, but if God says you can do it, you can. Your mind will say "stay mad at that person" but we need to live in the spirit, which is the Word, and the Word says to love and love covers a multitude of sins It takes practice. Once you do it, you will become addicted to walking in love. It is so nice to let people off the hook and be loving instead of trying to get even. When we stay mad at someone, we are only hurting ourselves.

We think we are letting people get by with something if we don't get even. Everyone has to give an account for their lives (*Romans 14:12*). If someone is mistreating you, trust God to work it out. Don't take God's job in your own hands. Walk in love and do your part and God will do the rest.

This will not happen overnight by reading my book. You must renew your mind to the Word of God (*Romans 12:2*). You must study Jesus' character and practice this. Read the scriptures over and over-- keep at it and love others as Christ loves you. Read *First Corinthians 13:4-8* and see what love involves.

We are being very selfish if we stay mad at someone. We are self-centered if we only think about how we feel. Always consider the other person. We have no idea why people do what they do. Hurting people hurt people. Do the right thing by loving people no matter how they treat you. If you want to have a victorious life, you must obey God. If you want to impact someone else's life, you must obey God and love people. You may have to be uncomfortable in order to help someone else. Can you imagine the impact Christians would make in this world if they would do what Jesus said to do? We have to quit being concerned about how someone is treating us and take the high road and love the unlovely. We will win people to Christ and be so joyful. Take the challenge and love. You can't do it on your own. Look to Jesus as your example. He will help you.

Love Is Power

Walking in love is power. If anything gets the devil mad it is being good to people who are not nice to you. The enemy wants you to be offended and stay mad at people who mistreat you. Take the high road and love. By being offended, you will be robbed of your power and anointing. You will block the flow of God's blessings by staying mad at someone. When you forgive, you are actually setting yourself up for a huge blessing.

God's ways are so different from the world's way. Our mind cannot make sense why we would let someone off the hook if they were rude to us. We want to get even or argue to make a point. We want to let someone know how we feel. We want to let them know that what they did hurt us. But God says to bless those who persecute you, bless those who are cruel to you (*Luke 6:27-28*). He says to overcome evil with good (*Romans 12:14,21*). We can't judge the person. We don't know why they are behaving the way they are. Love covers and judgment exposes.

God loves us when we do something wrong. He doesn't judge us and send punishment from heaven. Who do we think we are? We must learn to love like Jesus. We must love unconditionally. We are self-centered if we think about what people are doing to us. Quit focusing on yourself and look to Jesus. Figure out what you can do for someone that's hurt you. Are you willing to make a sacrifice and do something that doesn't benefit you? Why not forgive and love that person as God does and instead of getting mad at them, pray for them. Do something nice for them. Who knows why people do what they do? Leave them in God's hands. Show them the love of Christ and pray that they would know His love as well. You may be the only "Jesus" they will ever see and by being good to them you can be their connection to heaven. They can be born again and go to heaven instead of hell just because you showed them the love of God.

Give

We live in a selfish world today. Television, billboards, and magazines advertise many things that are tempting people. They'll say things like, "you deserve it" and "everybody else has one". We have become a 'what about me' society. That is a tragedy. I used to be very selfish and would never think of volunteering my time without getting paid. I never thought about giving ten percent of my income to a church. There was no way I was going to do any of that. When we live like that, we are into ourselves and we also are in charge of taking care of ourselves as well.

When you follow God's way, you will find out that He is your Provider.

> *"For from Him and through Him*
> *and to Him are all things."*
> *Romans 11:36 (NIV)*

> *"And my God will liberally supply (fill*
> *to the full) your every need according to*
> *His riches in glory in Christ Jesus."*
> *Philippians 4:19*

You can't expect God to bless you if you are not a giver. A great example is this: if you don't plant any corn seed, you won't have any corn. I hear many people praying for finances but they have not planted any seed. They haven't planted the Word of God in their heart and haven't given financially to their church or to help a friend. You must sow a seed to reap a harvest. That is God's Law of sowing and reaping. When we give, we will reap.

> *"Give, and it will be given to you. A good measure,*
> *pressed down, shaken together and running over,*
> *will be poured into your lap. For the measure*
> *you use, it will be measured back to you."*
> Luke 6:38 (NIV)

This is such an awesome promise. When you give, God will give back to you in abundance. If you plant one corn seed, you will have one stalk of corn with many seeds. If you plant a whole acre of corn seed, you will have an abundant amount of corn. The promise in *Luke 6:38* says that you will have so much, you will have to press it down and then shake the container until it runs over. God keeps His Word when you do what He says to do--love people, treat them right, forgive and be a giver. Our concern should not be what we can get from God or people, but what can we do for Him who first loved us? God doesn't need our money but He asks us to give because it is good for us. We have to do it by faith and God is faithful to keep His end of the deal by giving back to us what we have sown.

We are to give God our tithes. That is a tenth of our gross income. Here is the instruction in *Malachi 3:10 (NIV)*:

> *"Bring the whole tithe into the storehouse, that*
> *there may be food in My house. Test Me in this, says*
> *The Lord Almighty, and see if I will not throw open the*
> *floodgates of heaven and pour out so much blessing*
> *that you will not have room enough for it."*

Is that an awesome promise or what? When we bring our tithes to God, He will pour out a blessing back to us that we won't even have room for it. And this will not just be financial blessings but blessings in all areas of our lives. God works through people and you will begin to see blessings in every area of your life and live a life of fulfillment that is beyond words. The tithe is our divine connection to the Blessing.

You may say, "I don't know how I could ever give ten percent of my income? I can't even give one percent". That is where you have to give by faith. You may not be able to give ten percent right now but God says, "Test Me". When you are faithful to God, He is faithful to you. Give something--even if it's a pair of shoes in your closet. Give them to someone in need. You want to get to a point where ten percent isn't enough and you up that to a higher percentage. Be a radical giver and God will take care of you. Give your tithe and be a blessing wherever you can.

Give over ten percent and you will be radically blessed and give on top of your tithe to help others. Alms is talked about in *Matthew 6:1-4* which is giving to man out of compassion. This is helping the poor and is over and above your tithe. *Proverbs 19:17* says, *"He who has pity on the poor lends to the Lord, and that which he has given He will repay to him."* God will pay you back what you give to help people in need. We have to use discernment when it comes to people in need, but if the Holy Spirit says to give, we should obey. It is not our job to judge that person, it is our job to obey God. Sometimes you may not give money but be prompted to tell that person about Jesus or even ask them if <u>they</u> have anything to give. Then pray for them and tell them to expect a blessing from God.

The biggest harvest God promises is through the sowing of a seed. The Word of God is seed that we plant in our heart. The way we do that is by renewing our mind to God's Word. His Word is your only connection to the spiritual realm. More about this later on in the book. By sowing a financial seed you can reap up to one hundred fold. We are blessed through the Covenant of Abraham, Isaac, and Jacob (*Genesis 17:7, Galatians 3:16*). The covenants were made to Abraham and his Seed which is us who have faith in Christ. Seed is above your tithe and alms. Sowing a seed is where you are giving by faith expecting a harvest. You sow into fertile soil for it to yield an abundant harvest. An example of fertile soil is a ministry that is preaching the full Gospel and seeing souls saved. As a believer in Jesus Christ you are heirs of the Covenant. When you sow into good soil and expect a harvest, you will reap. God is faithful. God promises us a 30, 60, and even a hundred times as much. *Mark 4:8* says this:

> *"Still other seed fell on good soil. It came up,*
> *grew and produced a crop, multiplying thirty,*
> *sixty, or even a hundred times."*

God can also tell you to buy a piece of land that looks barren. I've heard of a guy doing this. The land didn't look like much but he felt prompted to buy it. Eventually the state built a highway through that land and offered him millions of dollars. If God says buy this or buy that, do it. If God says sow a seed, do it. Abraham's son, Isaac sowed seed during a famine and he received a hundred times as much as he had planted and the Lord blessed him (*Genesis 26:12*). Praise the Lord! God is able to take a barren land and turn it into the Garden of Eden. Sowing a seed is the answer for taking you over the top to help God further His Kingdom.

God wants His kids blessed to show that He is faithful to His promises (*Psalm 92:15*) and to show that God dwells among us (*Deuteronomy 28:10*). It is time for Christians to receive all that God has for them and operate in the power of Jesus. Many ministries get criticized because the preacher is very wealthy. If that ministry is operating under integrity and honesty then God promises to bless His kids. Who can help the poor if you don't have any money? Who is going to listen to a broke preacher? King Solomon who was the richest man that ever lived and ever will live said this in *Ecclesiastes 9:16*: "*Wisdom is better than strength: nevertheless the poor man's wisdom is despised and his words are not heard."(KJV)* Would you rather listen to someone who is broke or listen to someone that is wealthy and following Jesus?

When I was growing up, I thought ministers were poor. That sure didn't make me want to follow God. But when you find out what the Word says and know that He has such a good plan for you, you will change your thinking and begin to walk in the blessings of God and people will take notice. You will not have this blessed life if you do not get in the Word and do what God says to do. You will not have this life if you are stingy and tight with your money. Begin to tithe by faith and eventually give on top of your tithe and see that God is faithful. Heaven has streets of gold so why would God want us living like paupers here? Quit being religious and let's start showing the world who the real El Shaddai-the God of more than enough is.

He Paid The Price

As I said in the beginning of this book, Jesus Christ died so that we can have prosperity. We are to be prosperous spiritually, mentally, socially, physically, and financially. Christ paid a huge price and it is a shame when we only receive the forgiveness of our sins and toss the other promises aside. I think it is a slap in the face to God. If someone offers you a gift and you say, "Oh, I can't accept that. I'll take the bow off the box but I can't accept any more than that." What an insult. God wants us to receive all the promises He has for us and financial prosperity is one of them.

Many people think that Christians are to be poor or just comfortable. They think it is selfish to want money. It <u>is</u> selfish to only want enough for yourself. We are not to love money but we need money to live and to bless others. *First Timothy 6:10* says, *"For <u>the love of money</u> is a root of all evils…"*. It doesn't say money is the root of all evil. I have heard this misquoted ever since I was a kid. We are to use money to bless people, not use people to get money. How can we be a blessing to others if we are broke? It is really an ignorant way of thinking. Listen to what the Apostle Paul wrote in *II Corinthians 8:9 (NIV)*: *"For you know the grace of our Lord Jesus Christ, that though He was rich, yet for your sakes He became poor, so that you through His poverty might become rich."* Read all of *II Corinthians 9*. God wants us to give cheerfully and to have our needs met and to be enriched in every area of our lives so that we can be generous helping others. This will bring forth thanksgiving to God and to show that God dwells among us. He wants us to be an advertisement of His goodness.

Just Give Something

We need to give financially but there are so many other ways to give as well. Give your time to someone. Maybe it's a lonesome neighbor that lost their husband. Give her a ride to the grocery store. Make her dinner. Do something. We have got to quit being so selfish and quit thinking of only ourselves. If you're standing in the grocery line, buy the person's groceries that is behind you. Buy lunch for the car behind you in the drive thru line at a fast food restaurant. Give your time, your money, or your personal possessions, just do something. When you take care of others, God will take care of you.

Forgive

Not only do we have to love those that hurt us but we must forgive. I know what you may be thinking, especially if someone has done a horrible thing to you. I have heard testimonies of people who forgave the person that killed their brother or child. They actually become friends. That is the love of Jesus at its best.

If you have watched the movie, "The Passion of the Christ", you see the part toward the end where Jesus says, *"Father, forgive them, for they know not what they do."(Luke 23:34)* Think about that when someone has hurt you. If Jesus, who was persecuted and beaten beyond recognition can forgive those that tormented Him, we surely can forgive someone. <u>Quit feeling sorry for yourself and grow up</u>. Feeling sorry for yourself for what someone has done to you is selfish. Get over it! Quit blaming other people for the way your life turned out. You have choices so make the choice to forgive and move on with your life. Quit getting offended every time someone mistreats you. Offense is rampant everywhere and it is also rampant amongst Christians. How can we be a witness for Christ with an attitude like that? We must come up higher. We must take the high road and forgive. God forgives us everyday for the stupid things we do, surely we can do the same.

> *"Be gentle and forbearing with one another and, if one*
> *has a difference (a grievance or complaint) against*
> *another, readily pardoning each other; even as the Lord*
> *has [freely] forgiven you, so must you also [forgive]."*
> *Colossians 3:13*

You may say, "Surely, you don't expect me to forgive my father for beating my mother and me?" I am not making light of anyone's situation. There are many injustices in this world and we can't understand why these things happen. You must consider that hurting people hurt people. If that happened, have you ever thought about how your father was treated as a child? Maybe his father did the same thing to him. You have to decide if you are going to allow that to carry from generation to generation. Be the Christian and forgive. You are setting yourself free by forgiving.

This takes time and only God can heal your wounds. This is where you work with the Holy Spirit to reveal what you need to work on. You need to go to the root of the problem. If you have a problem with this, you will need to study forgiveness and mercy. Study Jesus and how He forgave. Love is not a feeling but an action. We don't feel like forgiving but if God says to do it, we can. But only with His help. We can't do it alone. We have to find out what God says to do.

> *"But I tell you who hear Me: Love your enemies,*
> *do good to those who hate you, bless those who*
> *curse you, pray for those who mistreat you."*
> *Luke 6:27-28 (NIV)*

"Now you've gone too far--love my enemies and bless them? Are you kidding?" I didn't say it, Jesus did. Those are His words and we must obey. Is it easy? No. But if God says to do it, then we can do it with His help. Another word for 'bless' is to speak well of. We need to shut our mouths and quit talking about it.

*"Do not let any unwholesome talk come our
of your mouths, but only what is helpful for
building others up according to their needs,
that it may benefit those who listen."*
Ephesians 4:29 (NIV)

I like to say, "If you can't say anything good, don't say anything at all." When someone mistreated me in the past, I would talk about it for weeks and maybe longer. I would think up ways to get even. What future is there in behaving like that? That is the way the world acts and we need to be the example to the world.

"What if a person that hurt me won't talk to me or they act like what they did to me wasn't a big deal?" Pray for them. Talk kindly to them and about them. Don't take the devil's bait of offense. Believe God will change their heart and make them aware of what they did. But even if they never acknowledge what they did was wrong or never apologize, forgive them and love them and move on. Declare that you have a loving relationship. You will have what you say (*Mark 11:23*). Be kind and treat them well.

You may have to be the first to apologize when you don't feel like it. If the Holy Spirit says to apologize even if it wasn't your fault, do it. Humble people will be the first to apologize. You will feel so much better if you do. What does it matter if it wasn't your fault? We have to get over thinking that someone is going to get away with something. Do the right thing.

Are You Mad At God?

Many people cannot only forgive someone who has wronged them but many Christians are mad at God. They ask, "God, why is this happening to me? Why is this person at work treating me like this?" If you are the only Christian where you work, why not take the challenge and be loving toward those that are treating you bad? "God, why did my father have to leave us? How could you allow that to happen?"

There can be many reasons someone is mad at God. God does not cause bad things to happen to us but He does promise that all things work together for good to those who love the Lord and are called according to His purpose (*Romans 8:28*). He works the things out that are in His Word. You can get on track with God and start to do things His way and seek His wisdom in all things. What has happened to you may not be good, but if you do what God says to do it will work out better than you can imagine. God is the last person you should be mad at. If you are mad at God, that will stop your fellowship with Him. It is impossible to have a relationship with someone you are mad at. God will always love you. He's not mad at you. We may not understand things we go through but there is always a way out. And Jesus is the Way--the only Way! If you are mad at God, repent and allow Him to teach you about His unconditional love for you so you can also love others unconditionally.

Forgive Yourself

You may also have to forgive yourself. Maybe you've had an abortion or you've cheated on your spouse. Maybe you are a veteran and have done things during war time that you feel shame or guilt over. Jesus Christ paid the price for your sin over 2,000 years ago. You do not have to pay the price of your sins over and over. *Romans 6:14* says this:

> *"For sin shall not [any longer] exert dominion over*
> *you, since now you are not under Law [as slaves], but*
> *under grace [as subjects of God's favor and mercy]."*

Jesus died for the sins of the whole world (*I John 2:2*). He took the punishment so you don't have to. He died for the sins of your unsaved neighbor. We have no right judging unsaved or saved peoples sins. God loves them and has forgiven them. The only sin people will be judged on is not believing in Jesus. Forgive others but now you need to forgive yourself. Many people are born again and think they have to behave perfectly or they are not worthy of having a relationship with God. As you can see in the above scripture, the sin you committed no longer can have a hold on you. Sin no longer has any power over us. "Does that mean it is okay to sin because I know God will forgive me?" As the Apostle Paul said, "Certainly not" (*Romans 6:15*). Your born again spirit will not want to sin. As you see how good the Father is to you, you will want to obey Him because He is not the mean taskmaster people make Him out to be.

He's not only forgiven your past sins but future sins as well. Many people don't preach this. Some are born again and know their past sins are forgiven. Then something happens and they sin and think that God won't forgive them. Jesus doesn't have to go to the cross all over again. He paid the price for every sin you have ever committed or will commit in the future. Think about it.

Make The Decision And Forgive

Not forgiving God, yourself, and others holds you in bondage. You have a choice to either forgive or remain in bondage. That choice is yours. Know that if you choose not to forgive, you are going against what God wants you to do. He never asks us to do something we are incapable of doing. Maybe you are holding onto your guilt because you feel you need to suffer or you don't deserve to be forgiven. You think no one has ever done anything as bad as you have. The work of Jesus Christ has already been done and you need to move on and start enjoying your life. God wants that for you. That is why He sent His Son to the cross. Don't play God or deny His gift to you. Receive His forgiveness. Forgive yourself. Don't let the enemy keep winning in your life. Ask yourself, "Do I want to please God or the devil?"

The Apostle Paul had done terrible things before He followed Christ and later continued to be persecuted for being a follower of Jesus Christ. If anyone should feel guilty about his past and bitter while he was being persecuted, it was him. But he said this in *Philippians 3:13-14*:

> *"I do not consider, brethren, that I have captured and made it my own [yet]; but one thing I do [it is my one aspiration]: forgetting what lies behind and straining forward to what lies ahead,* 14 *I press on toward the goal to win the [supreme and heavenly] prize to which God in Christ Jesus is calling us upward."*

Paul knew the importance of forgetting the past. He said to do <u>one thing</u> and that was to forget the past and strain to what is ahead. Prior in verse 10 of Philippians chapter three he said that his determined purpose was to know Christ and to know the power outflowing from His resurrection. Christ took our place and we are dead to anything that has happened to us or will happen to us. Make a decision to know Christ intimately and live the life Jesus died to give you.

Forgetting the past is the most important thing we have to do. If we hold on to the past, whether it is not forgiving ourselves, God or someone else, it will hold us in bondage. It will affect your prayer life. People die an early death because of guilt or unforgiveness toward someone. We are to press in to what is ahead. If we have to press then there is some work that needs to be done. We need to be determined to know Christ and what He has already done for us. We need to do things His way so that we can have the life that He died for us to have. Quit being so stubborn and think you have to pay or that someone else has to pay. <u>Jesus already paid</u>. Grow up and get over it. Think about someone else for a change. If you are consumed with guilt, you are concentrating on yourself. If someone has done something to you, pray and release them to God. God will deal with them in due time. Get to know Jesus and receive all He has for you. Do yourself a favor and follow God's way. <u>Receive His love for you.</u>

Not forgiving will stop the power and anointing in your life. Unforgiveness and offense will block the flow of God's blessings. Think about that! Strife is the devil's tactic to rob us of everything God has for us. If you can forgive someone of what they did to you, whether it is talking bad about you, any kind of mistreatment, or stealing from you, you will be amazed what God can do. Sow that offense or financial loss as a seed and believe God for an amazing blessing.

When you are a believer in Christ, you will be persecuted and have many opportunities to hold things against the person or people persecuting you. Read *Luke 6:22-23*. Jesus said we are blessed when people do evil, mean things to us. Verse *23* says that we are to leap for joy and be glad when people mistreat us. We can receive amazing blessings and power by letting everything go and love those who hurt us (*John 6:35*). What an amazing way to live.

As I was writing this book, we had a situation where someone had scammed us on the internet. It was a strange deal but long story short, we got robbed of $6,900. That's not a lot of money and I know that many people have had millions stolen, but hear my point. When my husband told me it was a scam, I was mad but immediately went to the Word and know that God hates robbery and He will repay. We forgave that person that stole from us and prayed that they would know Jesus. We sowed that money as a seed and believed God for our harvest. I'm excited to see what God will do. I know He is faithful. We actually were joyful and praising God and looking forward to our harvest.

We would both laugh and did not let the devil get a foothold. As I said before, any offense will rob you of your power and anointing. Find out what God says to do. Forgive immediately and watch your Daddy show up and show out.

Chapter 3

Renew Your Mind

*"Do not be conformed to this world (this age),
[fashioned after and adapted to its external,
superficial customs], but be transformed (changed)
by the [entire] renewal of your mind [by its new
ideals and its new attitude], so that you may
prove [for yourselves] what is the good and
acceptable and perfect will of God, even the
thing which is good and acceptable and
perfect [in His sight for you]."*
Romans 12:2

There are many Christians who are living in two worlds. They are living with one foot in the Kingdom of God and the other foot in the world. This way of living will not be prosperous. You will go to heaven if you've made Jesus Christ your Savior but you will not enjoy the journey on earth. There is a better and higher way to live. To find out what that way is, we have to renew our mind to the Word of God. We need to change our way of thinking then we will change what we believe and will speak what God says in His Word. Our thoughts and ways do not lead us to victory as God's way does. His thoughts and ways are higher than ours (*Isaiah 55:8*). We must read the Word and allow God to reveal to us the way we are to live. The Bible is our instruction manual for a prosperous life. If you're smart, you'll want to totally transform or change your way of thinking to God's way of thinking. *Joshua 1:8* says, *"This Book of the Law shall not depart out of your mouth, but you shall meditate on it day and night, that you may observe and do according to all that is written in it. For then you shall make your way prosperous, and then you shall deal wisely and have good success."*

After reading that scripture, you may say, "I need to meditate on the Bible day and night? I have to read the Bible constantly? How can I have a life?" The word 'meditate' means to think on one thing and to ponder. To ponder means to think about. If you are having a financial trial, roll over in your mind that God liberally supplies all your needs according to His riches and glory in Christ Jesus. Say that God loves you and He is your Provider. As you read His Word, you will see He has already provided everything you will ever need.

In order to replace your thinking with God's Word , you need to spend time in the Word. You need to read and study for yourself, listen to tapes and sermons, and watch Christian television. If you spend two hours a day watching soap operas or mindless TV, how about switching to reading the Bible and/or listening to someone who can teach you the Word of God? Why not listen to a CD while you are in the car on your hour commute to work and back? You will go from thinking about your problems to thinking about God's promises and His way of living and doing things. When you change from your old way of thinking to thinking like God thinks, then you will make your way prosperous and have good success. The end of *II Corinthians 10:5* says to lead every thought and purpose away captive into the obedience of Christ (the Messiah, the Anointed One). We can literally keep our minds on the Lord and His Word. We have a battle going on in our mind and if you are new to renewing your mind to the Word of God, you will have to deal with your old way of thinking. But pretty soon you will replace your old way of thinking with the Word of God and think His thoughts and do things His way. You listen to the Holy Spirit and involve Him in everything and consult Him on everything. He is much smarter than we are and then as it says in *Joshua 1:8* we will have much success and also keep our minds at peace when we have them stayed on the Lord and His Word (*Isaiah 26:3*).

If God says you can do this, then it can be done. The Lord told Joshua that he should meditate on the Word of God day and night. Moses had just died and Joshua got the job of leading about two to three million people into the Promised Land. If Joshua had time to meditate on the Word, you and I certainly have plenty of time.

The best thing I learned was to study an area I was having trouble with. My biggest problem area was worry. I looked up scriptures on worry and memorized them. Start with one to three scriptures and memorize them. When your thoughts go into negative mode, you speak the Word of God out loud and combat those negative thoughts. Instead of thinking and saying what the enemy says, say what God says in His Word. Over time you will begin to meditate on the Word day and night. The Holy Spirit will bring things to your remembrance. He is your Teacher.

You have to decide how much time you want to invest. Are you satisfied with your present life? If you are living in the world I doubt very much that you are one hundred percent happy. And if you are a Christian with one foot in the Kingdom and one foot in the world, you are fooling yourself if you are a hundred percent happy. If that is the case, you are putting value in your money or getting satisfaction out of a high position job. God wants us to put our trust in Him and not our money. Money is temporary but trusting God is eternal.

Your circumstances are going very well right now, but when tragedy hits you fall to pieces because God's Word is not sown in your heart. His promise that He always causes you to triumph is not what you stand on (*II Corinthians 2:14*). <u>If you allow your joy to be dictated by your circumstances, you are not spiritually mature.</u> Your joy is not found in your circumstances, it is found in Christ alone. Jesus has taken care of everything.

I know many people that are in a great mood when everything is going good, but then the next day something happens and they are crying and negative. They go by their circumstances and how they feel verses what the Word says. Most of the Christians I know live like this. They are no different than the people that are in the world and it is my conclusion that they are not baptized in the Holy Spirit and renewing their mind. Most are carnal Christians with a mind of the flesh which *Romans 8:6* says is sense and reason without the Holy Spirit. But they say, "Oh, I've got faith." Faith comes by hearing the Word of Christ (*Romans 10:17*) and most are hearing a watered down version of the Gospel. Most go to a church where they don't teach about Jesus and the baptism in the Holy Spirit and praying in tongues. God is a spirit and the connection to God is through His Word. The majority do not get the Word of God in their heart. If you don't receive the baptism in the Holy Spirit and become filled and controlled by the Spirit then you are powerless and will not have the life God has for you. You will live by your circumstances. You may go to heaven but will not see signs and wonders on the earth. How many churches are seeing signs and wonders? How many churches are laying hands on the sick and seeing them recover or casting out demons as Jesus talked about in *Mark 16:17-18?* Most churches are missing the power which is the Holy Spirit (*John 7:39*). Many are teaching from their mind. They may have knowledge of the Bible but what they are teaching doesn't give life to your spirit.

We are a spirit, we have a soul, and live in a body. I asked a Christian once how they thought they were connected to God and they said, "body, mind and soul". This was a person from a church I was going to for a season and they did not teach what I'm teaching you here. So that person didn't know any better. But what a tragedy to not even mention the Spirit. It is my personal experience that praying in tongues is evidence that you have been baptized in the Holy Spirit. You may receive the baptism in the Holy Spirit and not speak in tongues for two years. Just keep asking God and speak by faith. Don't give up! Bottom line is this: if you aren't living heaven on earth and in a good mood every day despite of what happens to you, then you are not living the life Jesus died to give you. You are carnal and not baptized in the Holy Spirit. You are not renewing your mind with God's Truth and your life will not be a witness to the people around you. This takes time and I am not criticizing you if you are a Christian and not happy everyday. Keep renewing your mind and you'll get there. I just see countless Christians not operating in the power of God. It is time for Christians to wake up and read the Bible for themselves instead of believing their pastor.

Jesus said this in *John 7:38, "He who believes in Me [who cleaves to and trusts in and relies on Me] as the Scripture has said, From his innermost being shall flow [continuously] springs and rivers of living water."* Then in the next verse (39) says, *"He was speaking here of the Spirit, Whom those who believed in Him were afterward to receive."* The disciples received the Holy Spirit and this power on the day of Pentecost (*Acts 2:1-4*) and began to pray in tongues. They began to see signs and wonders just as when they were with Jesus. This is for us today and without the fullness of the Holy Spirit you will not have power. If you have a natural river of living water, there is life and water can generate power. This river of living water is the Holy Spirit and tongues is the result. You will have the same power that raised Jesus from the dead. You will see people healed and delivered when you pray. You will live a victorious, powerful life that can affect everyone around you.

When you put your trust in God, receive the baptism in the Holy Spirit with the gift of tongues, and renew your mind to His Truth, your life will be wonderful and you will be a huge blessing to others.

What Are You Believing For?

I meet many Christians who do not spend much time in the Word of God. Many go to church and read their Bible once in a while. This makes them feel good. We don't receive by our good deeds, we receive blessings by God's grace (*Romans 11:6*). People are okay in life as long as things are going well. Then when trouble hits, they crumble. They are not renewing their mind with the Holy Spirit's help. They are not getting God's Word sown in their heart. People need to get their armor on and come against the enemies tactics. The Word of God is our armor (*Ephesians 6:11*). The Word is our protection from the enemy. If you don't know the Word of God you won't know what God has for you. How can you have any expectations other than what you see in front of you (your situation)? If you don't read the Word, you won't have faith for the supernatural. Faith comes by hearing the Word of God (*Romans 10:17*). If you only go by what you see in the natural and cry out to God to fix your problems, you're a carnal Christian (going by your five senses). A spirit filled Christian that meditates on the Word of God day and night lives in the promises of God and will see God results. If the doctor tells them they have cancer and will die in three months, they go to the Word and stand on what God says and believe by His stripes they are healed.

I used to just believe in God and figured I was on my own. I would go to church once in a while to feel good. I thought I would go to heaven but didn't realize the importance of renewing my mind to change my way of thinking. I was like a fish out of water flopping around in life with no direction or guidance. I lived like the world lived and it showed. My life was not producing any fruit. I thought by going to church once in a while, I was getting brownie points with God. I didn't know the importance of forgiving someone who had wronged me. I had no idea of the Law of sowing and reaping. I wasn't giving any of my money away to anyone, let alone a church.

So what was I believing for? I don't really know. I guess just a ticket to heaven.

Like I said in the beginning of this book, I believed that when I died I would go to heaven and that God created us to see what we could accomplish here. I had no idea the Bible was my manual on how to be a blessing to other people or that the Word of God was written for me to learn to think like God and believe what He says and do what He does and have what God says I could have. I had no idea that the Word of God could change me and fix every area of my life. In no way did I know that Jesus Christ bore my sicknesses and pain and became poor so that I could become rich (*Matthew 8:17 & II Corinthians 8:9*). We are to do exactly what Jesus did-raise the dead, lay hands on the sick, cast out demons, and see amazing miracles <u>today</u>!

I would see small town preachers that lived a modest life. Their life didn't look very inviting to me. The preacher who was barely getting by was not a life I wanted. I wanted to party and do crazy things. I didn't want to follow a bunch of rules and be poor. That was my impression of people that followed God.

Once I listened to some of the preachers on television and saw the lives they lived, I wanted to know more. Their lives were positive and prosperous. I had a wrong view of who God is. I thought those miracles were just for the disciples. I was living my life in the Old Testament and the New Testament. I believed an "eye for an eye". I believed that there were certain foods I couldn't eat. I believed it was a sin to work on Sunday. I thought Christians were poor and hypocritical. I didn't see any Christians lives that were bearing much fruit. My thinking was way off because I hadn't read the Bible for myself.

We Are Redeemed

It wasn't until I realized part of the Old Testament was under the Law and we as followers of Jesus Christ have been redeemed from the curse of the Law.

> *"Christ redeemed us from the curse of the law*
> *by becoming a curse for us, for it is written:*
> *Cursed is everyone who is hung on a tree."*
> *Galatians 3:13(NIV)*

Could that say it any plainer? The Old Testament is full of real life people who were blessed and overcame so much by following God. The Law did not come into affect until Moses. People were blessed under the Law but it depended on their performance. How much more can our lives be blessed under grace?

When we are born again, we begin to learn what God expects of us. We see what a blessed life we can have. We start to want to make changes in our life. That sin nature begins to fade and we see that the party life isn't all it's cracked up to be. We see that the world's way of living goes against living in the Kingdom of God. We now live under God's grace and we <u>want</u> to change. We don't change because we have to. God's grace is His power to overcome anything that comes into our life. We receive that through faith. We received salvation by the shed blood of Jesus Christ and we receive His gifts by faith. We receive <u>all</u> God's blessings by His grace through faith. We don't earn His blessings by what we do, we earn God's blessings because of what Jesus has done.

> *"For it is by free grace (God's unmerited favor) that you*
> *are saved (delivered from judgment and made partakers*
> *of Christ's salvation) through [your] faith. And this*
> *[salvation] is not of yourselves [of your own doing, it came*
> *not through your own striving], but it is the gift of God..."*
> *Ephesians 2:8*

> *"But He gives us more and more grace (power of the*
> *Holy Spirit, to meet this evil tendency and all others*
> *fully). That is why He says, God sets Himself against the*
> *proud and haughty, but gives grace [continually] to the*
> *lowly (those who are humble enough to receive it)."*
> *James 4:6*

Grace, as defined above in the amplified Bible, is the power of the Holy Spirit to meet this evil tendency and all others fully. The evil tendency here is that people are in love with the world (*James 4:4*). They are doing things on their own (the world's way) and not looking to God. But if you get rid of your pride and set yourself aside and know you can't do anything apart from Him (*John 15:5*), He will give you more and more grace. You can do things apart from Jesus but you won't bear the Kingdom fruit-the blessed life that God has for you. We don't have to do this alone--the Holy Spirit is our Helper, Teacher, Guide, and Comforter. With His help, you can do all things through Christ who strengthens you (*Philippians 4:13*).

"But the Counselor, the Holy Spirit, whom the Father
will send in My Name, will teach you all things and
will remind you of everything I have said to you."
John 14:26(NIV)

The Holy Spirit is a person and will teach you the Word. The Word of God will reveal to you that there is a higher way to live. We will be transformed by the entire renewal of our mind (*Romans 12:2*). We are made new creatures in Christ but still have things we do that are not pleasing to God. We will have to "tidy up" our life. There are things, like our thinking or things we do, that need reorganizing or fixing. You may be watching something on television and you feel you should not watch that anymore. The Holy Spirit will teach you a higher way to live. You don't live in bondage because you think God is mad at you because you do a certain thing. But God will show you a better way to live and things you did before don't appeal to you anymore. You change because you want to please God and live the life He has planned for you. You have a loving Father who has such a beautiful life for you and you appreciate Him showing you that better way to live. He shows you in such a loving and kind way. He speaks to you in a small, still voice (*I Kings 19:12*).

Our goal as Christians is to constantly strive to change our old way of thinking to thinking the way God thinks. We want to do things the way Jesus did and we will change over time. This won't happen overnight, but takes time by renewing the mind. You have to literally learn how to be a different person. I was a very selfish person before and had to learn how to love unconditionally and be giving as Jesus. You can't do this on your own. The Holy Spirit will reveal to you what you need to change and will help you. You can't get a deal like that anywhere. Hallelujah!

We have to forget the old religious sermons we may have heard. Many people are confused about the Old and New Testament. I've heard people who are born again say, "I don't feel like I deserve anything after what I've done. I'm a terrible sinner." They feel condemned about everything and can't seem to move on with their life. They don't know how to receive all the precious gifts from God.

They don't know they are forgiven and God has forgotten all their sins and remembers them no more (*Isaiah 43:25*).

Sin has no power over you. You are no longer an old sinner but a new creature. You are a child of God. *Romans 6:14* says, "*For sin shall not have dominion over you: for ye are not under the law, but under grace.*"(KJV) Once again, we have been redeemed from the Law and have inherited everything that Jesus is. God sees us the same way He sees Jesus (*Galatians 4:7*). We must get this and begin to live the life Jesus died to give us.

The only way these truths will become real to you is by reading the Bible for yourself. Look up the scriptures I have given you and study them. Meditate on them day and night. Renew your mind. Your natural mind isn't designed to believe God; it's your spirit that believes God. His Word is spirit and life (*John 6:63*). The Word of God is revealed to us through His Spirit (*I Corinthians 2:10*) which is the Word. *I Corinthians 2:9* says that eye has not seen and ear has not heard all that God has prepared for those who love Him. The Word doesn't make sense to our natural mind. You believe with your spirit. Verse *11* says no one can comprehend the thoughts of God except the Spirit of God. We can only know God through the spirit, not our mind. The Word of God has to get in your ears and in your eyes, then what's in your spirit will rule. We then think like God thinks, say what God says, and have what God says we can have.

When you receive the baptism in the Holy Sprit, the Word comes alive in you and becomes revelation knowledge. If you have not received His full power you will be limited and try to comprehend the Bible with your mind. Pray the prayer at the end of this book and receive His full power.

Renewing The Mind Brings Revelation

As I talked about in the first chapter of this book, we have inherited prosperity in every area, including financial prosperity, healing of our body, deliverance from oppression of any kind, and forgiveness of sins. Forgiveness of sins seems to be the Truth that most Christians understand. But healing of our physical body is the Truth that many dispute. One may say, "My mother died at 56 of breast cancer and I prayed that she wouldn't die."

There are things that we cannot explain but there are also things that we need to do being we have authority in the name of Jesus (*John 16:23*). If *Matthew 8:17* says that Jesus Christ took up our infirmities and carried our diseases, that means He took away **all** our diseases. I will discuss the power of words and believing prayer later. If you do not renew your mind to the Truth that all your diseases were put upon Jesus and *I Peter 2:24* that says, "*By His wounds we have been healed*", that will not be real to you. If you question healing at all, you won't have faith for it. The only way healing will become truth to you is to renew your mind to what God says. Your spirit has to overtake your soul and body for revelation to take place. The word 'revelation' means something that is revealed by God to man. Once God's Truth supersedes your five senses, healing of your physical body is the result.

Some say this is spiritual healing. Have you ever heard of a spiritual disease? The same way Jesus conquered sin is the same way He conquered sickness. Sickness came into the world through Adam's sin *(Romans 5:12)*. Jesus took care of both-sin and sickness *(Psalm 103:1-3)*. It's a done deal! This is so simple yet people will still argue that we won't be healed until we get to heaven. You don't need to wait to be healed. You need to be healed here on earth so you can help people. You have a legal right to healing-take it! You have a legal right to Jesus Name. He is called Jehovah Rapha which means Healer. Fight for what's yours. Don't just accept whatever the enemy throws your way. Don't settle when the doctor says you have cancer. Use your authority and cast that out. Say, "Cancer, you have no legal right in my body. Cancer, get out of my body and cells be restored in Jesus Name. I will live and not die."

Most Christians live by the flesh which is living by your five senses. When you are born again your spirit is brand new (*II Corinthians 5:17*), and it comes in line with the supernatural realm. The Holy

Spirit lives in your new spirit. But your soul and body are not brand new. That is why you must renew your mind to God's Word.

We receive all the promises of the New Covenant but those promises will not become real to you unless you change your way of thinking to the way God thinks. If you had one million dollars in the bank and didn't know it, you wouldn't be any better off. Receiving the promises of God are the same way. If you don't know what the promises are, you can't receive them. You can't have faith for something you don't know about. We receive God's promises by faith, but they will not become real to you unless you find out what they are. The Word must be sown in your heart.

Being healed of the cancer that you have does not seem possible. You are going by what the doctor says and he is saying you have one year to live. What needs to be done is to renew the mind to the Truth that *"by His wounds you have been healed"*. You need to find out what God says about you being healed and confess those scriptures so they become part of you. You cannot go by what the doctor says but need to believe what God says. <u>You cannot speak what you have (sickness), you must speak the truth of God's Word (*by His wounds I have been healed*)</u>. Jesus is our Healer and His Name is above every name (*Philippians 2:9*). His Name is above cancer and poverty. His Name is above all sickness and lack.

I have heard of people that were told they only had a short time to live, but they did just what I'm telling you to do. They got their healing scriptures out and confessed them despite of how they felt. They saw themselves healed. They saw Jesus taking that sickness. They believed the Word of God over the doctors report and are still alive today after the doctor told them 25 years ago they had two months to live. They renewed their mind to the Word of God and what was in their spirit became manifest in their body. They sowed the Word of God in their heart, watered the seed (the Word) by confessing it out loud, and the result (harvest or fruit) was that they were healed. I want to mention that you won't be healed by just repeating "by His stripes I am healed". You need to believe what the Word says and what's in your spirit will take over your soul and body.

Change Your Mind

We want to line up our thinking with God's. When you renew your mind to the Word of God, you will find out the will of God for your life. Read the end of *Romans 12:2* again and see that it says, *"… so that you may prove [for yourselves] what is the good and acceptable and perfect will of God, even the thing which is good and acceptable and perfect [in His sight for you]."*

This all may seem foreign to you. It was for me. But when you renew your mind to God's way of thinking, you will begin to see victory in your life. The will of God will be revealed to you (*Romans 12:2*). *Jeremiah 29:11* says, *"For I know the plans I have for you,"* declares the Lord, *"plans to prosper you and not to harm you, plans to give you hope and a future."(NIV)*

Everything about God is positive and everything about the devil is down and negative. We have to begin to renew our mind to a new way of thinking and then we will see prosperity in every area of our lives. People will want to know what you are doing because you are prospering and not moved by the circumstances in your life. And that will happen because of God and His help, not because we are some super, positive human being.

When you renew your mind and know that God always causes you to triumph (*II Corinthians 2:14*), there is nothing that will move you. You are secure and grounded on the Rock, which is Jesus Christ. You know that God has all the answers. You will then affect other peoples lives and that will start a chain reaction and get this country back in line with the Christian heritage it started with. We can then go to other parts of the world and tell people about our precious Jesus. Let's bring as many people to heaven as we possibly can. Let's renew our mind and receive all that God has for us so we can help someone else. Are you with me? Let's change our thinking and give the devil a nervous breakdown. The devil was defeated over 2,000 years ago and we as born again Christians need to take charge and walk in our authority over him (*I John 3:8*).

Chapter 4

You Have Authority

In The Beginning

When God created the earth and man, He gave man dominion (control) upon the earth. *Genesis 1:26* says, *"And God said, Let Us [Father, Son, and Holy Spirit] make mankind in Our image, after Our likeness, and let them have complete authority over the fish of the sea, the birds of the air, the [tame] beasts, and over all of the earth, and over everything that creeps upon the earth."* Man gave that authority away to Satan in the garden (*Genesis 3*). God wanted that authority to come back to man and had to come to earth in a physical body, which was Jesus Christ, to have authority on earth once again. The devil has no power over anyone who is born again. He has been defeated over 2,000 years ago.

> *"[But] he who commits sin [who practices evildoing]*
> *is of the devil [takes his character from the evil one],*
> *for the devil has sinned (violated the divine law)*
> *from the beginning. <u>The reason the Son of God was</u>*
> *<u>made manifest (visible) was to undo (destroy, loosen,</u>*
> *<u>and dissolve) the works the devil [has done]."</u>*
> *I John 3:8*

"Yet You have made him but a little lower than God [or heavenly beings], and You have crowned him with glory and honor. You made him to have dominion over the works of Your hands; You have put all things under his feet."
Psalm 8:5-6

I am amazed at the straightforward way God reveals His Truth to us. The more I read the Word, the more I see how plain everything is laid out for us. We have listened to preachers from our past who did not teach these things or we are currently going to a church where this has never been taught. Many Christians today are still allowing Satan to rule their lives. We were made a little lower than God, as *Psalm 8:5* says. God made man in His image meaning that we are to be like Jesus and do what Jesus did. We are His body and are to continue His work on the earth. Jesus came to reproduce Himself in us. People are living with guilt, depression, worry, strife, fear, anxiety, just to name a few. There is no need to do this. The enemy is the cause of this because people are not walking in their authority. Jesus said in *Luke 10:19*, *"Behold! I have given **you** authority and power to trample upon serpents and scorpions, and [physical and mental strength and ability] over all the power that the enemy [possesses]; and nothing shall in any way harm you."* If people don't know the Word and their authority, they will continue to allow the enemy to reign in their lives. The biggest area that the enemy has a foothold is in our mind. If you don't know the Truth of God's Word and you only rely on the enemies lies, you will live a defeated life. But Jesus destroyed the works of the devil. We must renew our minds to the Truth to live God's abundant life.

The Enemy Is Not Flesh And Blood

The enemy has been defeated but people are still letting him rule their lives. He is not a physical being with horns and a tail. The enemy is a spiritual being. The way the enemy works is through our thoughts.

*"For the weapons of our warfare are not physical
[weapons of flesh and blood], but they are mighty before
God for the overthrow and destruction of strongholds,
[Inasmuch as we] refute arguments and theories and
reasonings and every proud and lofty thing that sets
itself up against the [true] knowledge of God; and we
lead every thought and purpose away captive into the
obedience of Christ (the Messiah, the Anointed One)..."*
II Corinthians 10:4-5

As you can see in this scripture from *II Corinthians*, the war is not with physical bodies, like your neighbor or your co-worker, but the war is in your mind. The enemy works through people just like he worked through the serpent in the Garden of Eden. His main tactic is to deceive you. We can get these wild theories and ideas in our mind that the person in our office hates us. We can spend all of our time when we are off of work talking about that person and being miserable and they are enjoying their evening. Time is wasted getting distressed about maybe losing a job. People get fearful about their future and worry about their 401K not being there when they retire. We are worrying about something that may not even happen. Time is being spent being fearful and anxious in our mind when we could be reading God's Word and see what He has to say about our situation.

Worry pleases the devil and faith pleases God. We have to trust what the Word says. We cannot put our trust in people or our money but we can put our trust in God. He is always with us and will help us with everything (*Isaiah 41:10*). There is a solution for every problem you have. God's Word is full of solutions and positive answers. He does not want you to go by how you feel, what you hear, or what you see. He wants you to go by what His Word says. The Word of God is powerful to overcome anything that comes against you. But you have to actively fight against the enemy because he works in your mind.

Our physical body reacts to our thoughts. I have heard different percentages mentioned of how our thoughts are the cause of 85-95% of all illnesses. One person said it is more like 99% and I will have to agree with that. When you exchange your negative thoughts with the Word of God, you will begin to get healthier. *Proverbs 14:30* says, *"A calm and undisturbed mind and heart are the life and health of the body, but envy, jealousy, and wrath are like rottenness of the bones."* Any negative emotion is going to affect your physical body. Study *Proverbs 14:30* and see that the calm and undisturbed mind and heart are the life and health of the body. The body is affected so much by the mind. If your mind is worried, your body will be affected. Many diseases derive from negative thoughts--remember almost 99%. The devil is robbing us. But you don't have to allow him to control your life. We must replace the negative thoughts with God's Word.

You have authority and that authority is God's Word, the Blood, and the Name of Jesus. We have to take every thought captive into the obedience of Christ (*II Corinthians 10:5*). *Proverbs 4:20* says to give attention to God's words. What it boils down to is that we have to renew our mind, exchange our thoughts for God's thoughts, get them into our heart (not just our head), speak the Word of God out loud, trust God's Word and rest and receive His blessings. You will have what God has for you--forgiveness of sins, prosperity, healing, and the deliverance from every oppression. God's power is given to us in word form and using the name of Jesus gives us authority. When a couple gets married, the woman gets the husband's name. When we (the church) are born again, we too come to the Father in Jesus Name.

The Name Above Every Name

As a Christian, you have the same power and authority that Christ had. *Ephesians 1:19-20* says, *"And [so that you can know and understand] what is the immeasurable and unlimited and surpassing greatness of His power in and for us who believe, as demonstrated in the working of His mighty strength, Which He exerted in Christ when He raised Him from the dead and seated Him at His [own] right hand in the heavenly [places]..."* We have the same power Christ had and we are His body and we need to do the works that He did. *John 14:12* says that we will be able to do the same works and even greater works than Jesus did, which includes laying hands on the sick and casting out demons (*Mark 16:17-18*). The name of Jesus is the name above any sickness, fear, worry, lack and any power the enemy possesses. Sickness must bow to the finished work of Jesus.

> *"Therefore [because He stooped so low] God has*
> *highly exalted Him and has freely bestowed on Him*
> *the name that is above every name. That in (at)*
> *the name of Jesus every knee should (must) bow, in*
> *heaven and on earth and under the earth…"*
> *Philippians 2:9-10*

Tell Your Mountain To Be Gone In Jesus Name

You have to speak to your mountains in your life. Sickness and poverty are some of the mountains. You have authority in Christ when you receive the baptism in the Holy Spirit to lay hands on the sick. You have authority over sickness in <u>your</u> life. This definitely goes against what our mind thinks, but we have to do what the Word says if we want God results.

> *And Jesus, replying, said to them, "Have faith in God*
> *[constantly]. Truly I tell you, whoever says to this mountain,*
> *Be lifted up and thrown into the sea! And does not doubt*
> *at all in his heart but believes that what he says will take*
> *place, it will be done for him. For this reason I am telling*
> *you, whatever you ask for in prayer, believe (trust and be*
> *confident) that it is granted to you, and you will [get it]."*
> *Mark 11:22-24*

According to *Mark 11:22-24*, whoever says to sickness, be gone in Jesus Name, and believes what he says and doesn't doubt in his heart, it will be done for him. We will talk about this more in detail in a later chapter.

You might say, "this is getting too weird. I'm suppose to talk to my sickness?"

If you read the previous verses in *Mark 11:12-21*, Jesus spoke to the fig tree and cursed it. The next day when He and the disciples were walking by the tree, it was dead. Your mind has to be renewed to this way of thinking and speaking. We too have to speak to our mountains and cast them into the sea. It may not make sense to your mind but that is okay. It may not make sense, but faith will come and you will receive all that Jesus died for you to have. We have to do what Jesus did. We have to renew our mind. We have to sow the Word of God in our heart (*Mark 4:14*).

Our soul is our mind, will, and emotions. The mind is the way we think. The will is what we want. And our emotions are how we feel. Our soul needs to prosper and thrive. Our goal in life is to think like God thinks and say what God says. That is what God wants for us.

> *"Beloved, I pray that you may prosper in every*
> *way and [that your body] may keep well, even as*
> *[I know] your soul keeps well and prospers."*
> *III John 2*

Many times people will ask God to heal them. You have to realize something. That was done over 2,000 years ago when Jesus paid the price and took our sickness and pain in His physical body. If we are asking God to heal us, Jesus says to the Father, "Didn't we do that over 2,000 years ago? Did I go through all that for nothing?" You may not see results because it has already been done. You are in works of the flesh which is you trying to do something that is already done. Look at it like this: you are a healed body and Satan is trying to take that away from you. You must defend what is legally yours and that is to be healed. You have to take authority over your sickness and pain (*Luke 10:19*). If you are sick, you don't need to ask someone else to pray for you. You take authority in the Name of Jesus over that problem. *James 5:13* says, "*Is anyone among you afflicted (ill-treated, suffering evil)? He should pray.*" It doesn't say the pastor should pray. It doesn't say call

all your friends to pray. <u>You need to pray</u>. You need to exercise your authority. You can have someone lay hands on you but you can cast out your own sickness as well as lay hands on the sick. The next verse is saying that we should call in the church elders to pray. This verse is talking about people who are non-Christians or people who are feeble and bedridden, as someone in a coma. *Romans 8:11* says this:

> *"And if the Spirit of Him Who raised up Jesus*
> *from the dead dwells in you, [then] He Who raised*
> *up Christ Jesus from the dead will also restore to*
> *life your mortal (short-lived, perishable) bodies*
> *through His Spirit Who dwells in you."*

This may be talking about Jesus raising us up in the second coming but I believe He is also talking about healing our physical bodies today. If we have the same power in us that raised Christ from the dead (*Ephesians 1:19-20*), surely that same power has cured cancer, aids, and any disease that doesn't even have a name yet.

The Word Of God Is Armor

> *"Put on God's whole armor [the armor of a heavy-*
> *armed soldier which God supplies], that you*
> *may be able successfully to stand up against [all]*
> *the strategies and the deceits of the devil."*
> *Ephesians 6:11*

As you can see in *Ephesians 6*, the Word of God is your armor and gives you protection from anything the enemy throws at you. It will do you no good to just go to church once a week. You will need to study and confess God's Word and take authority. When fear comes against you, you need to speak *II Timothy 1:7* out loud and say, "God did not give me a spirit of fear, but of power, love, a calm and well-balanced mind and discipline and self-control." You need to combat that negative thought with the positive confession of God's Word.

Let's say that you are always concerned about your finances. (And I will say right here that I bring up finances a lot in this book because it is a huge problem today and the enemy is using the pressure of debt to destroy peoples lives). You work, but are living paycheck to paycheck. You are tithing to your church and walking in love but still in panic mode at the end of the month because you think you won't have enough money. Common sense, of course, is spending within your means. But if you are doing that, you need to get your armor on. Confess *Philippians 4:19*--God liberally supplies all of my needs according to His riches and glory in Christ Jesus. Believe the Word over the way it looks-the invisible over the visible. The supernatural over the natural circumstances. Your Father already knows what you have need of (*Matthew 6:8*). He is faithful (*Deuteronomy 7:9*). Relax and rest. *Hebrews 4:3* says those who believe do enter that rest. If you are not resting, you are not trusting in Jesus and His Word. You are going by what you see. If you are going to be victorious, you must believe the Word over your senses. You must be careful of what comes out of your mouth. Jesus said in *Matthew 12:34* that whatever is in your heart will come out of your mouth. So if you say you are trusting God and still saying, "Oh, I sure hope we get a big paycheck because we really need it. I hope God comes through". That is unbelief. If you are really in faith then you will say what the Word says no matter what it looks like in the natural.

Maybe you are a worrier. Jesus said in *Matthew 6:25*, "*Therefore I tell you, stop being perpetually uneasy (anxious and worried) about your life, what you shall eat or what you shall drink; or about your body, what you shall put on. Is not life greater [in quality] than food, and the body [far above and more excellent] than clothing?*"

Wow! Looks like God is telling us to rest and trust Him. A big problem with Christians is that they do not know the Word, and if they do, they are not getting these promises in their heart. They may have just heard this once in a while but haven't meditated on it and gotten to the point where they believe it and trust God to supply their needs. When are we going to believe what God says? I've heard it said this way--we are devaluing and dishonoring God if we worry. We are not trusting Him and His Word. We are praying and asking God to deliver us from things when God has already done everything. He has provided us with everything we need. He will liberally supply our needs and He has given us His Word to receive His blessing (*Psalm 3:8*) and given us the name of Jesus to take authority over any power the enemy possesses. The enemy is defeated. Done deal. But he will deceive you in your thoughts. Change your thoughts, you change your life.

It is futile to pray and ask God, "Oh God, please make our finances stretch until the end of the month". He already said in *Philippians 4:19* that He would supply them. If we are praying and begging then we are in unbelief. We need to thank God for what He has already provided for us. We need to take authority and command lack and poverty to leave our house in Jesus Name. We have to sow the Word of God in our hearts and speak the Word out loud and receive His blessings. Our prayer should be saying what God has said, agree with what He's already done, and thank Him for it. We need to come boldly to the throne of grace.

"Let us therefore come boldly unto the throne
of grace, that we may obtain mercy, and
find grace to help in time of need."
Hebrews 4:16

We have to come boldly to God and receive His blessings and thank Him for them. We are His children and He loves to shower us with His blessings. Jesus said in *Luke 12:32* that it is the Father's good pleasure to give us the Kingdom! And there was an explanation mark after it and I think He was saying this forcefully--"Believe this, trust Me!!" But He won't want to bless us if we don't receive. He won't want to give if we grovel and beg Him to meet our needs. He shouldn't have to push His blessings on us. But we first have to know what is ours through Christ. How do you like it when you give someone a gift that you spent a lot of money on and they say, "Oh, I can't take this, it's just too much"? You feel let down that they don't feel worthy to take your gift. That is how God feels. Jesus paid a huge price for us to receive all the blessings. We need to stand and take our authority and receive what rightfully belongs to us.

Chapter 5

Your Thoughts And Words Will Affect Your Life

The Power of Thoughts and Words

I'm sure you have heard the old saying, "Sticks and stones may break my bones but words will never hurt me." That is not true. We tend to remember the negative things someone has said about us over the positive things. If you were told as a child that you were no good and you'll never amount to anything, that more than likely stuck with you into adulthood. But someone that was brought up in a loving home with encouraging words will typically have a more positive image of themselves than the person who was told they were no good.

Words have a huge impact on us. Thoughts usually always turn into words. If you think something long enough it is going to come out of your mouth. Two very important scriptures in the Bible tell us the power that our thoughts and words have.

"For as he thinks in his heart, so is he..."
Proverbs 23:7

"A man's [moral] self shall be filled with the fruit of his mouth; and with the consequence of his words he must be satisfied [whether good or evil]. Death and life

are in the power of the tongue, and they who indulge
in it shall eat the fruit of it [for death or life]."
Proverbs 18:20-21

What we think and say about ourselves and our circumstances is very important. Many people don't even realize it but they are predicting their future whether it is positive or negative. Many are having today what they have said in the past. If you say, "I know I'll never get a good job", you probably won't. Maybe today you are dealing with an illness because you have predicted your future by what you've said in the past. You have said that because your family line has had diabetes you are sure to get it too. And now you have what you said. It is really quite simple. We don't think that our words will make a difference but they do. The Bible says very plainly, *"Death and life are in the power of the tongue"*. Your words will either speak death or life. The end of that verse says, *"and they who indulge in it shall eat the fruit of it"*. You will have what you say. If you say long enough, "I just know I'll never get married", you more than likely won't. And if you do, I pity the poor person that will marry you because you will carry that negative attitude wherever you go unless you renew your mind to God's Word.

If you say, "I'm so stupid", you are saying what God made is stupid. I challenge you from this day forward to begin to listen to yourself and pay attention to what you are thinking and saying. The Word of God is full of scriptures that say who you are "in Christ." Father God sees anyone that is born again the same way He sees Jesus. This is what God has to say to us.

"I in them and You in Me, in order that
they may become one and perfectly united,
that the world may know and [definitely]
recognize that You sent Me and that You have
loved them [even] as You have loved Me."
John 17:23

First John 3:1 says that we are the children of God.

*"See what [an incredible] quality of love the
Father has given (shown, bestowed on) us,
that we should [be permitted to] be named and
called and counted the <u>children of God</u>!..."*

Do you see what God says about us? He sees us as He sees Jesus. Anyone who accepts Jesus is a child of God. You are royalty and in right standing with Christ in the eyes of God (*Romans 5:17*). There are so many scriptures on who we are "in Christ". You need to begin to say what God says about you over anything negative your parents may have said. The only way to know what God says about you is to renew your mind to the Word of God. Your thinking must change from the negative impression you have of yourself to what God says about you. If you think bad thoughts, your words will reflect a negative life.

In Your Heart, Not Just In Your Head

The Word of God has to get into your heart before it will be real on the inside. The heart is your spirit and soul. We are a spirit, we have a soul, and we live in a body. Your soul is your mind (what you think), your emotions, (how you feel), and your will (what you want). When you are born-again, you receive a brand new spirit (*II Corinthians 5:17*). Everything that is true of Jesus is true of your born-again spirit. Everything we will ever need has been deposited into our spirit. But in order to get out what is in your spirit to your soul and physical body, you must renew your mind to the Word of God. Then what's in your spirit will manifest in your body and soul.

The Word of God is spirit and life (*John 6:63*). When the Word of God gets in your heart, which is your spirit and soul, and becomes revelation knowledge, then your spirit will dominate. You will no longer go by what you see, feel or think but will go by what the Word says. The Word is Truth and will lead you to the abundant life. You will begin to live by the Word of God. When your mind is changed to thinking and talking like God, your life will reflect it. *Matthew 12:34* says, "…*For out of the fullness (the overflow, the superabundance) of the heart the mouth speaks.*" If your mind is renewed to the Word of God that says, "*Praise the Lord, O my soul, and forget not all His benefits-- Who forgives all your sins and heals all your diseases…*"(*Psalm 103:2-3[NIV]*), then when the doctor says you have cancer you don't believe his report but you believe what the Word says. The Word says that Jesus Himself carried away our diseases. You stand on the Word and command that cancer to be gone in the Name of Jesus and are healed in your physical body. Jesus already provided healing for you over 2,000 years ago-it's already done. The same way He forgave your sins is the same way He healed your physical body. The physical has to submit to the spiritual. The spiritual realm is the greater force and is everlasting (*II Corinthians 4:18*). What's in my spirit is stronger than what I see, think, or feel. That's why we have to walk by faith and not by sight (*II Corinthians 5:7*).

The only way for this to happen is to get the Word of God in your heart and not just in your head. What happens is people live out of their head. When sickness comes, they panic and worry and talk about it because they have not renewed their mind to what God says. They don't have faith for healing because they don't teach that in their church. Well I'm telling you, find another church. Your life depends on it. People may have heard that God sometimes heals but they are deceived. It is always God's will to heal everyone. If you aren't healed, God is not the problem. It's us that is hindering what God has already done. But people go by what they see in the natural. We have to step into the supernatural to receive the supernatural blessings of God. When your mind is renewed to God's promise that Jesus bore all your diseases then you won't go by how things look but there will be a "knowing" that God's Word is true over what the doctor says. Healing may not be instantaneous. But don't give up. Meditate on Jesus-see Him carrying away your disease. Speak life, not death. See yourself healed and then suddenly one day your body will line up with the Word.

Renewing the mind takes time. It is not an overnight deal. You must take a scripture and chew on it. You must ponder and think about all that it says. For instance, *Matthew 6:31* says, *"Therefore do not worry and be anxious, saying, What are we going to have to eat? Or, What are we going to have to drink? Or, What are we going to have to wear?"* First of all Jesus is saying, 'Do not worry or be anxious.' So we know that we are not to do that. I was a worrier and this was one of the first scriptures I memorized. Jesus also said not to say "What are we going to have to wear?, etc. By picking apart this scripture, we can see many things here. We are not suppose to be worried about anything because God is our Provider. We will only know this if we have renewed our mind to His Word. God's got me covered and I'm not worried but resting. But if someone has not renewed their mind to this, they will just cry out to God and beg Him to help them. They will talk to their friends about their problem. The thing many Christians don't know is that God has already provided everything we need. We don't need to beg but believe and receive what He's already done.

Whatever is in your heart will come out of your mouth. Jesus said in *Matthew 6:31* is, *"do not worry and be anxious, **saying**"*. The minute we speak a thought we give it life. God will respond to our positive words and the devil will respond to our negative words. If we are worried about our finances, we need to say what God says. Instead of saying, "How are we ever going to make it this month?", I would say, "Thank you, Lord, that You liberally supply all of my needs according to Your riches and glory in Christ Jesus." If you are tithing and giving and loving people, God is faithful to keep His promise. His promise is when we give it will be given back to us and He will pour you out a blessing (*Luke 6:38 & Malachi 3:10*). When you do your part, God will do His part. If you are not giving, do not expect to get anything back. You can't have a harvest without planting a seed. You can get a miracle but you can't live on miracles. There has to be an exchange-- you do your part and God is faithful to do His part.

When you speak what God says instead of the negative things you used to say, you will see God results. Your angels can go to work when you speak the Word of God. *Psalm 103:20* says that *the angels hearken to the voice of His Word.* The Word of God spoken out loud goes to work in the spiritual realm. Your angels are going to work. Your negative words of worry and doubt also go to work in the spiritual realm but the devil will respond to those. You combat those negative words with the Word of God.

Everything starts with a thought. You have to be very careful and pay attention to your thoughts. Each morning before I get out of bed, I say, "This is the day the Lord has made. I will rejoice and be glad in it" *(Psalms 118:24)*. I set my mind and think God thoughts. *Colossians 3:2* says, *"And set your minds and keep them set on what is above (the higher things), not on the things that are on the earth."* I meditate on scripture. I confess the Word and confess the dreams that God has put in my heart. I pray in the Spirit and spend time with God. I communicate with Him all day long. We need to keep our thoughts on God and His Word and say what He says.

The Word Is Seed

Most of us were not brought up in a home where this was taught. Many believe in God and Jesus Christ but do not apply what God says to do. I did not know that I had to renew my mind. I grew up believing in God and Jesus but also thought and talked like the people in the world.

Being a Christian is really quite simple. God has provided everything that we need. But we must sow the Word of God in our hearts. God's Word has to be planted in our hearts like a seed has to be planted in the ground. Jesus said in *Mark 4:14* , *"The sower sows the Word"*. Jesus compares the Word of God to sowing a seed in the ground. Put seed in the ground, you will reap a harvest. Sow the Word of God in your heart, it will produce what it says.

When we renew our mind and have the Word of God in our heart and speak what God says instead of what it looks like, then we will be able to combat those negative thoughts and words with the life giving words of God *(John 6:63)*. The positive words of God will change our lives and we will begin to bear fruit *(John 15)*. Change in every area will be effortless. The promises of God will be received by grace, or a free gift from God, without struggle and effort. The grace of God is power. God has promises and we receive them by grace through faith. When we know the promises of God and they are in our heart, the 'rest of God' is the result (*Hebrews 4:3*). We enjoy our lives and are a huge witness to others around us. They will want to know the God that we serve.

In the natural, when you plant a seed in the ground, you expect a harvest. When we read and believe the Word, sow the Word of God in our heart, and confess the Word, we will reap a harvest as well. We must sow the Word, which *John 6:63* says the Word is spirit and life. The Bible is a spiritual book. God is a spirit and He created everything by words. If He had not spoken words, we wouldn't be here. We are a spirit, we have a soul and we live in a body. The only way to reap in the spiritual realm is to be spiritually minded which is walking by the Word of God.

This is how the Word of God works. We must sow it in our heart to bring about change. That is the work we do because God has already provided us with the outcome. It is amazing how the Word of God sown in our hearts has the ability to change your whole life. Jesus said that the Word of God is like a seed that is planted in the ground and our heart is the ground. In *Luke 8:15* He says this: *"But the seed in the good earth--these are the good-hearts who seize the Word and hold on no matter what, sticking with it until there's a harvest." (Message translation)* In *Marks* gospel, Jesus said this: *"God's kingdom is like seed thrown on a field by a man who then goes to bed and forgets about it. The seed sprouts and grows--*he has no idea how it happens*. The earth does it all without his help: first a green stem of grass, then a bud, then the ripened grain. When the grain is fully formed, he reaps-- harvest time!" (Mark 4:26-29 Message translation)*

We can't figure out how by believing that by His stripes we are healed brings healing to our physical body but it just does. Don't try to figure it out and analyze it. Just believe like a little child. Do what God says to do and you will live the abundant life He has for you. Many people that are highly educated will not receive this because they try to figure everything out--it just won't work for them. The word 'brainwashing' has a bit of a negative definition in Webster's. But if we were to use it in a positive sense with the Word of God, it is like we are washing our brains and lives with the water of the Word and it cleanses us of our old thoughts and negative thinking. Our lives begin to change and we live that abundant life that Jesus died for us to have. And we receive that life by sowing the Word of God in our hearts. Hallelujah!

What comes out of our mouth will affect our harvest. If God has put a dream in my heart but I still worry and say, "I don't know if God will ever open doors for me. This is just too hard." Nothing will happen. I am digging up my seed. My prayer is negated. The Word of God has not been sown in my heart. Jesus talks about this in *Mark 4*. He talks about how people hear the Word in different ways and compares the various ways to sowing a seed in the ground in different conditions. Sometimes people hear the Word but the enemy snatches it away because it was only what I would call 'surface listening'. You hear something but it doesn't sink in. You may forget it five minutes later. You must meditate on the Word of God day and night (*Joshua 1:8*). You must mutter it over and over again. You must study it and then it becomes part of you. You believe the Word over your circumstances and what you see in the natural.

God responds to our faith and faith in His Word. God responds to our positive confession of His Word, not our grumbling and complaining. Jesus is the High Priest of our confession (*Hebrews 4:14*). Jesus has been sent to carry out the words we say.

God doesn't want us just to go to church and hear a sermon once a week. Nothing can be planted in your heart by only hearing something once a week. So many people may hear the Word and have it in their head but not in their heart. They are not speaking God's Word, they are speaking what their head is saying. God wants us to be blessed. We are to seek first the Kingdom of God and His ways of doing and being right (*Matthew 6:33*) and sow the Word in our hearts and the promises of God will come to pass. Jesus said this in *John 15:7*:

> "If you live in Me [abide vitally united to Me] and <u>My words</u> remain in you and continue to <u>live in your hearts</u>, ask whatever you will, and it shall be done for you."

Think About What You Are Thinking About

Each morning I set my mind on God and His Word. I decide what I am going to think about. If I slip, the Holy Spirit reminds me of *Philippians 4:8*, which I have sown in my heart, and it says to "*think on what is true, worthy of reverence and honorable, think on whatever is just, and pure and lovely and lovable, whatever is kind and excellent and whatever is of good report* (various translations). I get rid of the negative thoughts and think on what is good and of a good report. You see, if you don't know the Word of God, you will not be able to exchange your negative thinking with God's positive words. What people do is pray and beg God to change their situation. He wants us to take responsibility with our thoughts and words. There has to be an exchange-we do something and then God does His part. He wants us to sow the Word of God in our heart and then we will see a harvest. Our lives will bear fruit (*John 15:4,8*). He has already provided prosperity, healing, and the deliverance from all oppression. He has already done His part. Now it is up to us to learn to think like God and say what God says to receive all God has for us.

I used to spend days and even months thinking about certain things that were going on in my life. My thought life was consumed with negative thoughts. I had no idea I could decide what to think about. When I found out this truth in God's Word, it changed my life. As I covered a little bit in chapter four, our thoughts have a negative or positive affect on our physical body. *Proverbs 14:30* says, "*A calm and undisturbed mind and heart are the life and health of the body, but envy, jealousy, and wrath are like rottenness of the bones. Proverbs 17:22* says, "*A happy heart is good medicine and a cheerful mind works healing, but a broken spirit, dries up the bones.*"

Look at the negative affect a disturbed and worried mind has on the body. Pay attention to your body and thoughts. If you feel tense in your neck or back, you may find out that you are worried about something. If you have neck or back problems or irritable bowel syndrome, take a look at your life and see what you've been thinking about or saying. Maybe you are holding unforgiveness toward someone. Your negative thoughts can be a root cause of your physical ailments. But when you have a calm mind renewed to the Word of God, you will be healthy in every way. I believe 95 to 99% of illnesses stem from our thoughts. Pay attention to what you are thinking about.

Sometimes I hear of a person that is not very old and they die of cancer. I've heard it said like this: "She was only 45 and such a good person." But what do we really know about her thoughts? Was she unhappy inside? Did she cover up some pain from her past? We don't know. There are some things we just can't figure out so don't try. Sickness is from the devil and her thoughts are what could have brought on that cancer. Remember *Proverbs* says an undisturbed mind and heart are the life and health of the body. But we live in a fallen world and some things you just can't figure out. Don't even try. <u>But always remember--God is not the cause of death and destruction.</u> The devil is (*John 10:10*). If it's good, it's God and if it's bad, it's the devil. Period!

Speak The Word And Not Your Problem

Speaking the Word instead of the problem has changed my life. I pay attention to what I say. I very seldom allow any negative words to come out of my mouth. I understand the power that my words have in the spiritual realm. I hear people say things like, "I just love her to death" or "I bet I'll never find a job". These things are not smart to say. We have to pay attention to what we are saying.

The Word of God is powerful. God spoke the world into existence with His Words (*Genesis 1*). Everything that was made, God spoke into existence. The scripture says, "*And God **said**, Let there be light; and there was light (Genesis 1:3).* Light was not just zapped into the atmosphere. Light was created by the spoken Word of God.

We too have the ability to speak what we say into existence. If you say long enough, "I'll always be broke, my mamma and daddy never had anything, so I know I won't either". You will have what you say. But if you say, "The Blessing of the Lord is upon me and the

Blessing makes me rich" (*Psalm 3:8 & Proverbs 10:22*), you will have that. Now this isn't some name it, claim it thing. I hear that a lot. If it is in the Word, it is yours. You do have to do your part and speak what God says and in time you will have what God has for you. You will need to be obedient to God. You must walk in love, which is the new commandment (*John 13:34-35*). You can't expect to have what you say and treat people bad. God will bless those that are obedient to His ways. But always remember--we are righteous by faith not by our works or performance (*Romans 5:1*). We are obedient to God, not to get something, but because it is the right way. His way leads to a life that is better than we could ever imagine.

You may feel dumb saying you are blessed and the blessing makes you rich when you are broke, but you have to speak what the Word says and not what you see in the natural (*Romans 4:17*). In the spirit, you are blessed. Keep sowing the Word in your heart and doing your part and God's blessings will come to pass. You must speak God's promises by faith even when things look impossible in the natural. That's why you have to walk by faith and not by sight (*II Corinthians 5:7*). That's why we must believe in a supernatural God over what we see in the natural.

This worked for Abraham. God told him he would be the father of many nations when it looked impossible. Abraham and his wife were way past child bearing years and in the natural it looked impossible for them to have a baby. But God said it would happen and Abraham believed God. See what *Romans 4:17* says about this.

> *"As it is written, I have made you the father of many nations. [He was appointed our father] in the sight of God in Whom he believed, Who gives life to the dead and speaks of the nonexistent things that [He has foretold and promised] as if they [already] existed."*

God spoke this to Abraham when it looked impossible. He spoke of something that was nonexistent as if it already existed. Bearing a child looked impossible to Abraham, but the seed was planted and all

Abraham had to do was believe. Abraham and his wife called each other the father and mother of many nations long before they saw any evidence of it at all. The King James Version says in *Romans 4:19* that Abraham did not consider his own body that was as good as dead nor did he look at the deadness of Sarah's womb. He <u>only believed God</u> and not what things looked like. I love that. That is faith. And he is our example. We also need to be assured that <u>God is able</u> to keep His Word *(Romans 4:21)*.

If a woman gets pregnant, you can't see any physical evidence at first. She has announced that she is pregnant because the doctor has confirmed conception because the seed was planted by her husband in her womb. They are telling everyone by faith even though there is no physical evidence showing.

There are things in our life that don't look so good. Maybe you have given and tithed and been walking in love and it looks like you are going to go under. But when you speak the Word of God out loud and confess *Philippians 4:19* and <u>believe it</u>, God is faithful to come through. The physical has to submit to the spiritual. It may not be in your timing, but your financial breakthrough will come. You have to keep speaking what God says and not talk about the way it looks in the natural. You have to speak something that is nonexistent as if it already exists. When God promises something, it will happen. The Word of God sown in your heart will bring you the harvest. Keep speaking the Word and be patient until the seed breaks ground. <u>Keep confessing the end results not the present circumstances</u>. "Thank you, Lord that you are faithful and liberally supply all of my needs".

Patience is crucial and needs to develop. *Hebrews 10:36* says, *"For you have need of steadfast patience and endurance, so that you may perform and fully accomplish the will of God, and thus receive and carry away [and enjoy to the full] what is promised."* Through faith and patience you will inherit the promises *(Hebrews 6:12)*. That's what faith is all about. Faith is believing what God says. Jesus said to come like a little child. Children believe things easily. Don't make it complicated. Enjoy your life while God is working. Speak what God says and relax and let God do the rest. He is faithful!

Take Authority With Your Mouth

Many Christians, and I mean <u>many</u>, do not know they have authority over the devil. They do not know he was defeated over 2,000 years ago. Christians are not taking their authority. They are allowing their circumstances to dictate their life.

> *Behold! <u>I have given you authority and power</u> to trample upon serpents and scorpions, and [physical and mental strength and ability] over all the power that the enemy [possesses]; and nothing shall in any way harm you."*
> *Luke 10:19*

The end of *I John 3:8* says, *"The reason the Son of God was made manifest (visible) was to undo (destroy, loosen, and dissolve) the works the devil [has done]".* The devil has no power over us in our thinking, our circumstances, or in any way, shape, or form. So why do so many Christians allow him to run their lives? People are depressed, worried, fearful, afraid of losing their job, fearful of the economy, and allowing sickness to ruin their lives. Jesus has undone the works of the devil. Jesus has given us His name (*Philippians 2:9*). What more do we want? The problem is many do not know this and have been taught incorrectly. Study these scriptures and begin to take authority over Satan. Renew your mind to what God promises you and speak to your mountains. Take authority with your mouth. As an example, you must speak to debt and lack. You must tell it to get out of your house. Command lack to be gone in the Name of Jesus. Sounds silly but Jesus spoke to the fig tree (*Mark 11:12-21*).

> *And Jesus, replying, said to them, "Have faith in God [constantly]. <u>Truly I tell you, whoever says to this mountain, Be lifted up and thrown into the sea!</u> and does not doubt at all in his heart but believes that what he says will take place, it will be done for him. For this reason I am telling*

you, whatever you ask for in prayer, believe (trust and be
confident) that it is granted to you, and you will [get it]."
Mark 11:22-24

Look at what Jesus said in *Mark 11*. "*Truly I tell you, whoever says*
to this mountain, Be lifted up and thrown into the sea! It can't get any
plainer. Speak to your mountain and tell it to be gone and into the
sea.

If we have sickness come upon us, we need to take authority over
whatever is attacking us. Sickness and pain are from the devil and we
have authority over him. We need to tell that pain in our side to be
gone in Jesus Name and not live by how we feel but live by the Word
of God. The Word of God has to overtake the way we feel. We need
to walk in our authority and take charge. God has given us His Word
and the Name above every Name (*Philippians 2:9*). We need to quit
bowing down to the devil and put him in his place which is under
our feet (*I Corinthians 15:25*). *Mark 11* says it best. We need to speak
to our mountains and our mountains can be sickness, debt, and lack.
We need to meditate on healing scriptures (I have some at the end
of this book). See Jesus taking your pain and sickness. The end of
Matthew 8:17 says that *Jesus Himself took [in order to carry away] our*
weaknesses and infirmities and bore away our diseases. See Him carry
away your pain and disease. Take communion, pray in tongues and
stand against the devil and fight for what is rightfully yours (healing).
Matthew 11:12 says that the Kingdom of heaven suffers violence but
the violent take it by force. Fight for what Jesus did for you.

We should not have to pray long prayers. We should be able to
pray the Word, believe, receive, and rest. It is really quite simple but
people do not know this truth. Instead of praying, "Oh, God, please
bring us the money we need this month to pay our bills. We ask that
you would be so good to bring us the $200 we need." What you do
instead of begging is pray the Word and say, "Thank you Father that
you provide food and provision for us (*Psalm 111:5*) and thank you
Lord that You liberally supply our needs according to Your riches and
glory in Christ Jesus (*Philippians 4:19*). You know what we need. We

give You praise and glory that You are faithful. In Jesus Name, we believe and receive our blessings."

These are just a few promises that I'm talking about. There are so many promises in scripture that tell us how God has provided our needs. Also, many scriptures saying that God has healed our diseases. Search these out and confess them out loud. I have listed a few in the back of this book. Read them, confess them and get them into your heart. Believe the Word more than your circumstances. Sow the Word of God in your heart and your harvest will come. You do your part, which is believing (*John 6:29*), and God will do the rest.

You Reap What You Sow

I used to talk about my problem to anyone who would listen. I talked about it over and over again. I would think about my problem day and night. I thought that was the normal thing to do. I didn't know that I had control over my thoughts. I didn't know that what I was speaking was making the devil happy. I had no idea that I was sowing bad seed into the spiritual realm. I was giving the devil opportunity to work in my life. I did not know this truth about God's Word and did not live a very good life. I was not bearing any fruit. The end of *Galatians 4:7* says, "*...For whatever a man sows, that and that only is what he will reap*".

Sometimes we only think this in a monetary way. We think if we only give a dollar, we'll only get a little back. But this also pertains to our words. If we speak bad about someone, we are sowing seeds for us to reap. Maybe later on someone is saying bad things about us. Are we now reaping what we have sown? Being I talked bad about someone, are they now talking bad about me? Or we may be cursing someone else's future with the words of our mouth. Think before you speak.

Judgment

Judgment for me was a big problem. A couple of meanings for the word judgment is 'determine' or 'condemn.' *John 3:17* says, "*For*

God did not send the Son into the world in order to judge (to reject, to condemn, to pass sentence on) the world, but that the world might find salvation and be made safe and sound through Him."

As followers of Christ, we are not condemned when we do something wrong (*Romans 8:1*). Condemnation is from the devil. We have been forgiven (*Colossians 1:14*) of all of our sins-past, present, and future. God did not send Jesus into the world to judge us. Who do we think we are if we are going to judge someone else?

Do not judge and criticize and condemn
others, so that you may not be judged and
criticized and condemned yourselves."
Matthew 7:1

If we judge and criticize others, we can expect to be criticized and judged ourselves. Let's say a woman walks into church with a very short skirt and low cut blouse. She's got tattoos all over her body and pink hair. We think, "That isn't any way to come to church". What are we the fashion police for the church? There are things we do not know. We have no right to judge someone for their outside appearance. That woman has maybe been saved a month and loves God. God sees her heart and He does not judge her on her appearance. Maybe she needs to be more conservative in her dress so pray for her and allow the Holy Spirit to work in her life. You may be surprised to see her the next Sunday with a more conservative outfit on. If we were to condemn her, we would scare her off. Jesus spoke to and loved on anyone. I love how he spoke to prostitutes. No one was beneath Him. He did not judge and condemn someone for their appearance or their past behavior.

The end of *I Samuel 16:7* says, "*...For the Lord sees not as man sees; for man looks on the outward appearance, but the Lord looks on the heart.*" I know people who may not have good behavior or do everything they should be doing, but they have a good heart. They love God and He sees their heart. It is my place to love them because love always believes the best (*I Corinthians 13*). <u>Love doesn't keep score of the sins of others</u>.

I think judgment is rampant among Christians. I despise it when someone speaks negatively about others or makes fun of them. Have I done this? Absolutely. But I am very aware of reaping what I sow. I have no right to judge anyone. There are things I do not know about a person. What gives me the right to judge another because they aren't like me? Judgment is pride and God hates pride. It's not my job to judge someone else. God loves us unconditionally and He doesn't look at all of our faults and imperfections. Why do we think we can pick people apart and judge them? We cannot think bad thoughts in our mind or criticize someone with our words. It has to stop. Don't talk negatively about others. You will never be a witness for Christ if you do that. You are also opening a door for the devil as well.

Have I criticized other churches? That would be a yes on that too. There are churches that do not preach the full Gospel but I am going to appreciate our similarities and not dwell on what we don't agree on. I will pray that they come to know the full Gospel as Jesus wanted us to know.

We have to be careful what we think and say. *Psalm 34:13* says, *"Keep your tongue from evil and your lips from speaking deceit"*. We must begin to obey what God says to do so that we can be a good witness for Christ. Christians have a bad reputation for being rude and religious and that has to stop. I have work to do in this area so don't feel bad. It is something in our nature that we think because someone is not like us we can talk about what's wrong with them. We can judge whether something is right or wrong but we have no right to make a judgment against someone without knowing all they may be going through. Ask God to help you in this area and study scriptures that pertain to this. I like *I Corinthians 13:4-8* that says what love does. And the two that fit this best is, *"love believes the best of every person"* and love covers and judgment exposes.

Be Careful What You Hear

Not only are our thoughts and the words that come out of our mouth important but what we hear will also affect our lives. Jesus said this in *Mark 4:24*:

> And He said to them, "Be careful what you are
> hearing. The measure [of thought and study] you
> give [to the truth you hear] will be the measure [of
> virtue and knowledge] that comes back to you--and
> more [besides] will be given to you who hear."

Jesus is telling us to be careful what we are hearing. If you are not hearing the full Gospel, you will be limited in the power and knowledge of God. When you have revelation knowledge that God has healed you and prospered you, your life will be powerful. I will talk more about this scripture later on in chapter eight. The more we hear the Truth of the Word, the better. In *Mark 4:24,* Jesus is talking about God's Word and we will get out of it what we put into it. You will hear different doctrines--some are correct and some are not. Read the Bible for yourself. I use to hear that it was humble to be poor. I then read the Bible for myself and found out that God wants us to be blessed in every area. Ask the Lord for discernment on hearing His Word.

But we also need to be careful what we are hearing in general. If you listen to dirty jokes and gossip at work, you are acting like the people in the world. We need to stand out as Christians and take the high road. Now we don't have to say, "repent you sinners" and walk away from our co-workers, but we can politely say, "I really don't care to listen to dirty jokes". You can leave it at that.

We also need to be careful what we are hearing in our music and what we watch on television. Don't listen to music with cursing or negative impressions. Screen the music your kids listen to. Someone may say, "well I just like the beat". Those words still have an affect on you. I grew up in the 60's and 70's and I'll hear an old song that I used to listen to and be amazed at the content of it. I didn't even pay attention to those words back then.

What you watch on television or the movies you watch have a major affect on you. If you are watching mindless television with nudity and swearing, think about what you are gaining watching that kind of stuff. As Jesus said in *Mark 4:24, "the measure you give will be the measure that comes back to you"*. I know He was talking about the Word but really what are you gaining by watching a dirty movie? This will depend on what is important to you. Wouldn't you rather be reading the Word or watching a preacher on Christian television who can teach you how to walk in love? Instead of watching a TV show with evil witchcraft in it, you could be learning how to forgive that person at work who did you wrong. When you sow into the Kingdom of God, you will be blessed beyond your wildest dreams here on earth and in heaven.

You may say, "Can't I have any fun?" Being a Christian is very fun. You just need to change a few things in your life. The Holy Spirit will teach you. You will start to feel a little uneasy when you are watching that movie with bad language. You are the home of God and the Holy Spirit is grieved when we are doing things that are hurting us or others. *Ephesians 4:30* says, *"do not grieve the Holy Spirit"*. One definition for 'grieve' is intense sorrow. Like I said before, it all depends on what you want out of life.

I am passionate about God and His ways are not our ways. His ways are higher than our ways (*Isaiah 55:8-9*). I want to be a witness for Christ and I will not be one if I am watching foul and mindless things. I want to have a great life and be a blessing to others. God promises us a wonderful life but we do need to be obedient to Him. Being a Christian is so much fun. You may need to make a few changes and believe me it will be worth it.

I used to watch dirty movies and tell dirty jokes but I still believed in God. Would I have gone to heaven? Yes. Jesus was my Savior but He wasn't my Lord. I didn't let Him lord over my life. I was not respectful of Him. I didn't have the knowledge I needed and I was very selfish and only interested in myself.

If you've made Jesus your Savior you will go to heaven. If you have also made Him your Lord, He is your example. He is your authority and you want to learn His character and become like Him. You will want to give up your selfish ways and begin to give up the nasty things you do. Also, being baptized in the Holy Spirit will change you drastically. The Holy Spirit will get a hold of you and you will want to change.

What kind of life do you want to have here on earth? If we are living like the world, we are selfish. We are only concerned about ourselves. We may have to give up some things in order to be a witness for Christ. Are you just concerned about yourself and your pleasure? Wouldn't it be more joyful to live like the Word says and be a witness to people and have many come to heaven with us? It will be rewarding to be a witness to people so that others can also enjoy heaven on earth. We must take the narrow path. Jesus said in *Matthew 7:14, "But the gate is narrow (contracted by pressure) and the way is straitened and compressed that leads away to life, and few are those who find it."* Jesus is talking about people who don't believe in Him and that those people will go to hell. There is a larger amount that will go to hell than to heaven. What a shame but Jesus said it was so. I also believe that many that confess to be Christians are going on a path that will lead them to a lesser life. So many Christians are living with one foot in the world and one foot in the Kingdom. If you get both feet in the Kingdom and have Jesus as your example, imagine what life can be like. Your mind cannot fathom how wonderful it will be (*I Corinthians 2:9*).

Be careful of what you hear and what you watch. Be careful what you think and the words that come out of your mouth. *Ephesians 4:29* says, "*Let no foul or polluting language, nor evil word nor unwholesome or worthless talk [ever] come out of your mouth, but only such [speech] as is good and beneficial to the spiritual progress of others, as is fitting to the need and the occasion, that it may be a blessing and give grace (God's favor) to those who hear it.*" In other words, as I said before, if you can't say anything good, don't say anything at all.

Sow Comforting, Kind Words

The Bible has so much to say about words. Words have so much power. God spoke the world into existence by His words. It is amazing to me how many people don't think that what they say is a big deal. It is a very big deal. Your life depends on it.

> *"I call heaven and earth to witness this day against*
> *you that I have set before you life and death, the*
> *blessings and the curses; therefore choose life,*
> *that you and your descendants may live."*
> *Deuteronomy 30:19*

Your life can either be positive or negative--it is your choice. Your words do have consequences. We will have to give an account for the words that we speak. Jesus said this in *Matthew 12:36-37*:

> *"But I tell you, on the day of judgment men will*
> *have to give account for every idle (inoperative,*
> *nonworking) word they speak. For by your words*
> *you will be justified and acquitted, and by your*
> *words you will be condemned and sentenced."*

Maybe you don't care about the words you speak. But how about caring about someone else? What you say affects your children. What you say affects so many other people. As an employer, what you say to someone could be life or death. There are a lot of troubled people out there and instead of destroying them with our words, ask God for wisdom on how to approach people that need to be corrected or how to encourage someone that seems troubled. Pray for someone that was rude to you in the grocery store. Show them love and kindness instead of an insult. This can change our world. We hear of disturbed people that have killed innocent people for no reason. Many that knew a person like that say, "He was really a strange guy, nobody liked him". What if someone would have treated a guy like that with kind words or prayed for him? What a concept? This can make a huge difference in our world. We can be their only connection to God by being nice to them and praying for them.

Let's use our words carefully to encourage and edify (*I Thessalonians 5:11*). Let's sow comforting, kind words that could keep someone from committing suicide. Study love. Study the ways of Jesus. He was so kind and loving, yet firm when He needed to be. Let's speak life over someone, not death.

> *This is my comfort and consolation in my affliction:*
> *that Your word has revived me and given me life.*
> *Psalm 119:50*

Kind words comfort us. The Word of God comforts us. The Word revives us and gives us life. Begin to exchange your ways, your thoughts and your words for God's. Your life will begin to change. You will be happy, prosperous, healthy and in turn be a witness and blessing to others.

Chapter 6

Prayer

Prayer is powerful. Do we have any idea how powerful prayer really is? We can talk to God anytime we want. We can pray a prayer for someone that lives halfway around the world. We can pray for someone on the street and they don't even know it but their life could be drastically changed just because of our prayer. Prayer is releasing heaven to earth. I never really understood the power of prayer and only prayed when I needed help from God. After I did all I could do by myself, then I would ask God to intervene. Isn't that the way most Christians are? God is just there for an emergency? But God wants us to pray and pray about everything. He is our Heavenly Father and wants to help us in all ways. I see a major problem with most Christians. They are praying for something they already have.

As I said in the first chapter, God has already provided everything for us when we accept Jesus as our Lord and Savior. He has provided prosperity (*II Corinthians 8:9*), healing of our body (*Psalm 103:3 & Matthew 8:17*), deliverance from the oppression of the devil (*Colossians 1:13*), forgiveness of our past, present and future sins (*Colossians 1:14*), and eternal life (*John 3:16 & John 17:3*). We don't have to try and get all of this, we already have it all in the spiritual realm. We shouldn't be praying to try to get God to do these things. God gave us believers legal right to rule the earth. We take authority over any oppression, sickness, and poverty. We command sickness and pain to leave our body because it has no legal right to be there.

We need to renew our mind to find out what we already have. Then what is in our spirit will manifest in our lives. I had to also renew my mind to a better way to pray.

I had a major breakthrough when I found out my prayer is answered the minute I pray. You might say, "what do you mean by that?" I read *Mark 11:22-24* and my prayer life changed. In the previous verses, Jesus comes across a fig tree and the fig tree did not have any fruit. In a fig tree, the fruit appears at the same time as the leaves. But Jesus came upon the tree and He spoke to it. He said, "*No one ever again shall eat fruit from you.*" (*Mark 11:14*) He spoke to the fig tree. **He spoke to a tree.** That may seem odd but keep with me. That fig tree did not look dead the minute He spoke to it. He and the disciples came by about 24 hours later and the tree had withered away. Peter remarked that the tree Jesus spoke to had withered away. Jesus prayer was answered the minute He prayed but the manifestation of it (seeing it was withered and dead) showed up about 24 hours later. Look at what *Mark 11:22-24* says:

> *And Jesus, replying, said to them. "Have faith in God [constantly]. Truly I tell you, whoever says to this mountain, Be lifted up and thrown into the sea! And does not doubt at all in his heart but believes that what he says will take place, it will be done for him. For this reason I am telling you, whatever you ask for in prayer, believe (trust and be confident) that it is granted to you, and you will [get it]."*

First, Jesus is telling us to have faith in God not ourselves. He is not saying to have faith in what you see. He is not telling us to have faith in God if everything is going well. No, He is saying to have faith in God **constantly**. Not sometimes, but all the time. We must look at what we can't see instead of what we can see. If we look at what we can see, we will get discouraged. We must look to Jesus (*Hebrews 12:1-2*) and only to Him. If we take our eyes off of Jesus and analyze our circumstances, we are sunk. We have to believe in the supernatural power of God. We have to quit looking at things in the natural and look at the supernatural. The supernatural is what we can't see. If it looks like you are going to go under because your money is running out, you are looking at what you see with your physical eyes. But the Word of God says that *He will supply food and provision for those who reverently fear Him (Psalm 111:5)*. You can't see your situation changing but by looking at the Word, you are covered. God has put His "super" on your "natural". If He says He will provide food and provision, we must believe Him even if it doesn't look that way in the natural.

You must speak what God says instead of the way it looks. Begging Him is not going to get God to move because He's already done everything. But saying what God says will increase your faith. You believe more of what you say than anybody else. Faith must speak. God responds to faith and the devil responds to fear. What God says is the Truth and He is faithful. You must speak God's promises out loud. If God had not spoken when He created the earth or man, we wouldn't be here. If you don't speak God's Word, you won't see His promises come to pass. You can't make something manifest by just thinking about it. You must speak!

There is another time when Jesus prayed and the prayer was answered the moment he prayed. This is in *John 4:46-54*. There was a royal official whose son was ill. He heard about Jesus and begged him to come and cure his son. But Jesus didn't even go to where the boy was but just said, *"Your son will live!"* When the official was on his way home, his servants ran to him and said, "Your son lives!" He asked what time he had begun to get better and they told him yesterday. That was exactly when Jesus had prayed for him. The prayer was answered the moment Jesus prayed. If you get this, it will change your life.

Next in *Mark 11*, Jesus is telling us to speak to our mountain. Our mountain can be anything from sickness to debt to a spirit of selfishness in your child. I talked a little about this in chapter three. If you have a virus, say, "Father I thank You that healing has already been made available to me. Virus, in Jesus Name be gone and thrown into the sea. I receive my healing. I am healed". If your child is very selfish, you can bind that spirit of selfishness off of him. *Matthew 16:19* says, *"whatever you bind on earth will be bound in heaven and whatever you loose on earth will be loosed in heaven."* (shortened version) There is no sickness or selfishness in heaven so there is to be none on earth either. You can say (and you may not want to say this to your child's face), "I bind the spirit of selfishness off of Anthony, in the name of Jesus. I loose love on him, in Jesus Name. I thank you that salvation has already been made available to Anthony. I pray that he will have a desire to want to know You, Lord. Use me to help him know You. And if he won't listen to me, put someone in his path that he will listen to. I pray that he will come to his senses and escape out of the snare of the devil *(II Timothy 2:26)*. Thank You, Father". Anthony may still act like the devil, but you keep loving him and thanking God and declaring that Anthony is a loving and sweet son. You do this because your prayer has already been answered. You must look at *Mark 11:22-24* over and over again and allow the Holy Spirit to reveal this to you. Once you do, it's shoutin' time. This changed my life. Every time I pray, I believe I receive the answer when I pray. Then I thank God that my prayer is answered and I am resting while God is working. I confess the answer to my prayer as if it already happened. God is faithful to answer your prayer. Make sure it lines up with God's word.

I want to point out another important point that will make more sense to you. You don't get what you pray, you get what you believe you receive when you pray. There is a huge difference. Here is an example: If you pray for your daughter to come closer to the Lord and that someone will be put in her path that she will listen to about Jesus, then after you pray you must believe that that prayer is answered. No matter how she acts, if you continue to believe, God will put someone in her path that she can relate to and listen to (because she may not be listening to you), then what you prayed will manifest. You have a choice: you can pray that prayer and still worry about her and talk about her and what she is doing that isn't helping her or you can love her and trust God that He has already planned for your daughter to meet someone and she will fall radically in love with Jesus. When you believe what you prayed then you are praising God that your daughter is serving Him. You are rejoicing even though she still is acting the same way. You know God hears your prayers and will answer your prayer when you believe what you've prayed. Continue to love her, confess her serving the Lord, and leave it in God's hands. He has already answered your prayer. *Romans 8:31 says, If God be for me, who can be against me?* (shortened) This is when you sit back and rest and God can go to work. This is huge and changed my life. It makes perfect sense and this is how God wants us to live. He wants us to believe.

"How can I thank God for something that isn't true yet?" This is calling things that be not as though they are (*Romans 4:17 KJV*). Before Abraham was the father of many nations, he had to speak it by faith. He believed God when God told him he would have a child at his old age. It didn't look good in the natural for him and his wife to have a child but he believed God and spoke things that were nonexistent as if they already existed. Abraham saw himself as the father of many nations. He spoke with faith what he couldn't see with his physical eyes. He spoke what he saw in the spiritual realm. We are to do the same thing. Thank God for what He has already given you in the spiritual realm. Thank Him (don't beg) <u>everyday until your prayer has manifested</u>.

I hear people say, "I'm praying for my sick aunt. And, whatever God wants to do. Whatever His will is." Let's say your aunt if 42 years old. First of all, it is not God's will for us to be sick-Jesus took every sickness in His physical body. And it is certainly not God's will that someone die at 42. Quit saying if it's God's will. What you need to do is take authority over her sickness and cast it out. Tell her cancer to be gone in Jesus Name. God has already healed your aunt. Remember Psalm *103:3*? "*Who forgives [every one of] all your iniquities, Who heals [each one of] all your diseases.*" Jesus took our sickness and pain in His physical body .

People will pray and ask God to heal them. As I said in chapter three, He already did that over 2,000 years ago. We must take authority over pain and sickness. God can't give you something you already have. He gave **us** authority and dominion (*Psalm 8:6*) and He has given us His Word (*John 17:8*). Sickness is from the devil and people are letting the devil have full reign in their lives. If they get sick, they will baby their bodies and cater to its every need. Your spirit must rule over your five senses and that comes by being in the Word. Don't let your body rule you. Don't cater to its every need.

This is a major problem with Christians. Many are not taught this. They only think their sins are forgiven and they will spend eternity with Jesus in heaven when they die. They do not believe that Jesus took sickness away from us. They don't believe that we are not to be sick on this earth. You cannot have faith for something you don't hear. You must be baptized in the Holy Spirit and study God's Word. Faith will only come by hearing these truths (*Romans 10:17*).

"But you don't understand. My friend believed in Jesus and he died of cancer at 55". Did He believe that Jesus paid the price for his sickness? Did he know to take authority over that cancer and cast it into the sea despite of the way he felt? There are so many things that go along with this. You have to know what Jesus did for you. You need to know you have the same power and authority as Jesus did (*Luke 10:19*). We are to do on this earth what He did. You are just like Him when you are baptized in the Holy Spirit. You are empowered. Like I said, if you aren't hearing these truths, they will not be real to you. There are some who believed that Jesus took their sickness and still died. I cannot explain that. There are some things we just can't figure out. But I know it is not God's will for us to be sick. Jesus said in the Lord's prayer, "Thy Kingdom come, thy will be done. On earth as it is in heaven." There is no sickness in heaven. We are to take authority over sickness. And this is what woke me up in *Mark 11*. Knowing what you have already inherited in Christ (which you do by renewing your mind) and speaking to your mountain is key to victory in your life.

God has already provided everything we need. We need to receive it by faith and thank God for what He has promised us in His word. For instance, let's say it looks like you will be short at the end of the month to pay your house payment. If you are tithing and honoring God, you do not have to panic. If you know *Philippians 4:19* that says

God will liberally supply all of your needs according to His riches and glory in Christ Jesus, then you need to say, "Father I thank you that prosperity has been granted to me. I thank You that You supply our needs. And I thank you for the money to pay our house payment. Money, you come in in Jesus Name." But why would you say that when it looks like you'll be short? <u>Don't go by what you see, go by what the Word says</u>. God will make a way for you to have your mortgage money. Trust Him. You pray, believe, receive, thank Him, and rest. If we fail to believe until we see something, then that is not faith. Faith is believing in what you cannot see. And we don't tithe to get God to do something for us. Tithing is what God asks us to do so we honor Him with our money and He will take care of us.

A mistake people make is working hard to achieve success. They are working hard to make a living and not giving God the time of day. They are working with much toil and praying for God to meet their needs or praying for the money to make the mortgage payment or beg God to heal them. Salvation has been made available since the beginning. Salvation includes forgiveness of sins, healing of your physical body, financial provision, wholeness and prosperity in every area of your life. It includes protection and everything good. God is good and Jesus came so that we can have an abundant life on this earth (*John 10:10*). He wants us to have heaven on earth. Jesus is with us now-He lives in you when you are born again. We don't have to wait until heaven to enjoy life. People pray prayers that are powerless. They pray, "Oh God, please heal me. I'm so sick and don't know what to do." The right way to pray would be "Father, I thank you that healing has been granted to me and I trust that I'm not going to be healed **but I believe I am already healed**. I command this pain to be gone, in Jesus Name. I receive my healing right now." If you are begging God for something that He has already provided then you are getting into a 'works' mentality. You are doing something to get God to heal you. You are trying to get God to do something by trying to have more faith or getting 10 other people to pray for you. Faith is our positive response to what God has provided by grace. Jesus died over 2,000 years ago and He took your sins, sickness and poverty on Himself. He can't die again so that you can be healed, forgiven or prosperous. Seek Him and receive His grace (all He did for you). Receive everything by faith and quit begging God for what you already have. I hear people pray in church, "Oh God, come into this place." He said in *Hebrews 13:5* that if we are born again, He would never leave us or forsake us. I want to yell, "God is here--if I'm here God is here. I don't know about the rest of you." People say silly things.

Jesus said in *Matthew 6:33*, *"But seek (aim at and strive after) first of all His kingdom and His righteousness (His way of doing and being right), and then all these things taken together will be given you besides."* In the previous verses of *Matthew 6*, He is telling us not to be worried and anxious on what we will eat or wear. He tells us to look at the birds and see that they are not jumping around worried about what they will eat. They always have more than enough. What Jesus wants us to do is seek Him first, then everything will come effortlessly. You may say, "Am I suppose to just be carefree and not work to provide for my family?" No, that is not it at all. When you seek God first, your job will not become your source. God is your source. You will be working unto Him. You will do things His way. You read the Word, seek Him and follow God's ways, then everything you need will be added unto you. We don't seek Him to get stuff, we seek Him for Who He is. As you get into the Word, you will see that God gives you Wisdom and favor. He directs your steps. You will be amazed at how customers are calling you instead of you struggling and striving to make them buy from you. Seek God first and God will see that you have your needs met and doors of opportunity will open for you. It will be like the birds, only tons better. They are always taken care of. When you seek God first, you'll have everything you need.

The kingdom of God that Jesus talks about is mentioned in *Romans 14:17*.

> *"[After all] the kingdom of God is not a matter of [getting the] food and drink [one likes], but instead it is righteousness (that state which makes a person acceptable to God) and [heart] peace and joy in the Holy Spirit."*

The kingdom of God is righteousness, peace, and joy in the Holy Spirit. When you know that you are righteous because of what Jesus has done and you follow the leadership of the Holy Spirit, you will have peace and joy. When you know you are in right standing with God and have peace and joy in any situation, you will have everything you need.

You must abide in Him. Jesus said in *John 15:4, "Dwell in Me, and I will dwell in you. [Live in Me, and I will live in you.] Just as no branch can bear fruit of itself without abiding in (being vitally united to) the vine, neither can you bear fruit unless you abide in Me."* To abide means to stay, remain, and to be constant. We must learn to think how God thinks and look at the supernatural over the natural. We cannot bear fruit apart from Him just like fruit has to be on a tree to grow. An apple just doesn't appear. It has to be attached to a vine. We will not bear fruit if we do things apart from Jesus. We can bear fruit on our own but it will be with much toil. What we start on our own, we will have to uphold on our own. God is not obligated to help us if we do things apart from Him. When you seek God first, your needs will be met supernaturally. You don't need to go after stuff, you need to go after Jesus then you'll have everything you require and more on top of that. We want to have more than enough so we can give it away (*II Corinthians 9:6-15*).

When He talks about seeking God, He is not just talking about believing in God or going to church once in a while. You need to seek Him everyday. Be in His word everyday. You feed your body food, you need to feed your spirit the Word. Start by meditating on a scripture. Maybe you have a problem with your temper. Find a scripture on patience and meditate on it until it is in your heart. Then allow the Holy Spirit to reveal other things to you that you need to change. Focus on one thing at a time. You don't need your nose in the Bible 24-7. Even if you started with one scripture and meditated on it day and night. Roll it over in your mind and pretty soon it will get in your heart and you will become calmer and more peaceful. When you have a chance to lose your temper, the Holy Spirit will remind you of God's Word and you do what He says over what your flesh wants to do.

Your life can be so much more enjoyable and profitable by doing things God's way. And you will be a witness and blessing to others. You will not have to beg God to supply your needs. Your prayer life will be so much different. You don't have to beg for the things that God has already provided for you--healing, prosperity, and the deliverance from the oppression of the devil. If you pray for what you already have, that is unbelief. Seek God first and He will supply everything. Renew you mind to God's Word and find out what He has already provided by grace.

The next part of *Mark 11* says that we are not to doubt at all in our heart but believe that what we say will take place. We are to believe what we say, then it will be done. Let's say your employer is laying off some people. You've prayed that you would be able to keep your job. You thank God that He gives you favor because that's what it says in *Numbers 6:25*. You believe what you prayed for is answered--you keep your job. Then rest. Jesus said to believe and not doubt that what you say will take place. What people do is start saying things like this: "Well, I've prayed and I sure hope God answers my prayers. But Carol just got laid off and she's been here longer than I have." You are negating your prayer right there with your negative words. Jesus said you will have what you say. If you say the negative things, you'll have them. What people do is pray and then still talk about what they are seeing. They've asked for a positive result and negate the prayer with the words of their mouth. If you say you believe one thing and speak doubt out of your mouth, that is called double minded. *James 1:7-8* says that truly a person will not receive if he is double minded.

This works in any way, shape or form. Jesus said you will have what you say. If all you talk about is negative things, then that's what you will get. If you talk about how bad the economy is and don't know how you will make it and say you'll probably lose your business, then you will. People are predicting their future whether positive or negative or cancelling out everything with a little of both. You have to say what the Word says. What people do is pray and then still talk about the problem over and over again. Smith Wigglesworth, who was a great man of God in the late 1800's and early 1900's, said this: "We should recognize that our prayers are in vain unless we really expect what we ask to be granted to us." When we are double minded we should not expect to receive anything from the Lord. We are praying and asking God one minute and then talking about the problem the next. That is a prayer that is useless. As I said earlier, you don't get what you pray, you get what you believe you receive when you pray. There is a big difference. Pray your prayer, believe it is answered, don't waiver, and remain at rest. Praise God that your prayer is answered and suddenly God will come through. The only reason He wouldn't come through is that what we prayed is not best for a person and/or situation and we may not be praying the will of God. In that case, God is protecting us and has something better for us and Father always knows best.

People will also pray the same prayer over and over again. In *John 16:24 & Matthew 7:7,* in some translations, it says to ask in His Name and keep on asking and you will receive. But the King James Version, which I feel is the most accurate, says to ask and it will be given to you, seek and you will find, and knock and the door will be opened. We do not have to ask for the same thing over and over again. He is saying we can come to Him all the time. We thank Him for what He's already given us. We don't have to feel guilty because we ask for too much. God wants us to lean on Him entirely and we can keep asking but not about the same thing over and over. I hear many people say, "I'm praying for Mary every day". Pray your prayer and then thank Him for the answer. Thank Him every day that your prayer is answered until you see the full manifestation of that prayer. God heard you the first time you prayed. Why should we keep asking Him for what we prayed the first time? *Mark 11* says to believe what you pray is granted to you. If you pray the same prayer over and over again, you are acting as if God didn't hear you the first time and you are begging Him. You are actually in unbelief.

You see if you don't know the Word, you will not know how to pray. You will probably pray, "God, please bring us some money to pay our mortgage at the end of the month". He already said in His Word that He's supplied your needs. If you are praying and begging Him for the mortgage, then you are in unbelief. But this is how many people pray. They have not sown the Word of God in their heart. They don't know that God has already provided everything. If you already have a wife, why would you pray about getting a wife? You've already got one. You would be denying you have a wife. Simple but makes sense, doesn't it?

People may be praying for a financial miracle when they haven't tithed or given anything to anyone. You must sow a seed to reap a harvest. You can get a miracle but you can't live on miracles. We must do our part.

I hear people pray for peace or patience. God has already given you peace and patience. He has given you the fruit of the Spirit. You receive these fruits when Jesus comes to live on the inside of you.

> *"But the fruit of the [Holy] Spirit [the work which His*
> *presence within accomplishes] is love, joy (gladness),*
> ***peace, patience** (an even temper, forbearance), kindness,*
> *goodness (benevolence), faithfulness, gentleness (meekness,*
> *humility), self-control (self-restraint, continence)."*
> *Galatians 5:22-23*

If you know anything about fruit in the natural, you know it has to ripen or develop. An orange does not appear ripe on the tree. This takes time. The fruit inside of us takes time to develop as well. It is deposited on the inside of us but development of these fruits come through trials and tests in our lives. If you pray for patience, God will say, "You already have patience on the inside of you, so let's develop it". Things may come up in your life to develop patience. There may be a co-worker that is driving you crazy. They are like sand paper. There is your opportunity to develop.

Many people will run from these trials. They don't like someone at work, so they quit. I have done that on many occasions and looking back wished I would have known this and allowed my fruit to ripen. When you do things God's way, you will become more patient with every challenging person and/or trial.

The same is true for peace. Practice your peace. Pursue peace (*I Peter 3:11*). Stay peaceful when that driver cuts you off in traffic. Thank the Lord for that person. Thank God that you have an opportunity to develop peace and patience. When you look at it like that, the devil doesn't know what to do with you. Is that awesome or what? Listen to your prayers. Are you praying for something you've already got?

Jesus said in *Mark 11:24, "For this reason I am telling you, whatever you ask for in prayer, believe (trust and be confident) that it is granted to you, and you will [get it]."*

This is the Amplified version and see how Jesus said that whatever you ask for in prayer, believe (trust and be confident) that it is granted to you, and you will [get it]. He didn't say you might get your prayer answered or only if you are good will I answer your prayer. No, He said you will have your prayer answered. He says this on several occasions. See *John 14:13-14, 15:7, 15:16, 16:23, I John 5:14-15.* Right here are five references that say whatever you ask for you will receive. Jesus wouldn't have said this that many times if He didn't mean it and wanted us to get it. God wants us to be blessed. He wants our prayers to be answered. He wants people to see His power working on this earth. Always remember, if it is in the Word, you can have it. You can't just pray for anything.

Finally, Jesus tells us in verse *25 of Mark 11* that if we have anything against anyone, to drop it and let it go. If you are angry and have not forgiven some people in your life, this will hinder your prayers. It will rob you of the power and anointing and block the flow of God's blessings. God does not make bad things happen to you, but if your prayers are not being answered take a look at any unforgiveness you may have toward someone. Always remember how many times God has forgiven you. Let it go and forgive.

In *Mark 11:25-26,* Jesus said that if you don't forgive someone, God won't forgive you. This is where we have to rightly divide the word of Truth. Jesus preached the Law to the Jewish people when He was on this earth. But after His death and resurrection, we are now under grace and our sins <u>are</u> forgiven, past, present, and future. The end of *Ephesians 4:32* says that we are to forgive one another [readily and freely] as God in Christ **has forgiven you.** So if we hold unforgiveness toward someone and we believe in Jesus Christ, God has forgiven us. Our holding unforgiveness toward someone will hinder our power, blessings, and everything in general. Even our health will be affected (*Proverbs 14:30*). **The devil wants you to stay in strife--don't take his bait--FORGIVE!**

Praying In Jesus Name

Praying in Jesus Name is very important. God has given us the Holy Spirit. The Holy Spirit is the third person of the Trinity. Jesus sacrificed so much for us and God the Father wants us to receive all the blessings. He wants our prayers to be answered and they can only be answered by the Name that is above every Name. We come to Father God in the Name of Jesus. We have a personal relationship with the Almighty Creator of heaven and earth through Jesus Christ. We cannot come to Him or have a personal relationship in our own name or in someone else's name. All authority and power has been given to Jesus. Jesus said in *Matthew 28:18*, "*All authority (all power of rule) in heaven and on earth has been given to Me.*" We receive that power by confessing Jesus as our Lord and Savior and being baptized in the Holy Spirit. God comes to live in us through the Holy Spirit (*Colossians 2:10*). When we are in Christ, we are filled with the Godhead-Father, Son and Holy Spirit. Our born again spirits are identical to Christ's spirit. We then become one of God's kids. He sees us the same way He sees Jesus. And we come into God's presence through the blood of Jesus and all authority and power of God are given to us by confessing Him as Lord (*Romans 10:9-10*) and by speaking His Name. We have authority through His Word and we have victory through the Blood (*Romans 3:25*).

When a woman gets married she will take her husband's name. She will also receive everything else that her husband has like a car, money, house, etc. When we become children of God, we also receive the Name of Jesus and all that Jesus has. Jesus is not sick, broke, or oppressed by the devil. So neither are we. Anything that comes against us, we take authority over it in the Name of Jesus. As I talked about in the past chapters, we must renew our mind to this because it does not make sense in our head.

It is so important to **not** use the Name of Jesus flippantly. Honor and respect go with His Name. We cannot just use His Name casually or when we are frustrated. Be mindful of watching movies that do not respect God's Name or the Name of Jesus.

Our prayers of faith will have power by praying in Jesus Name. Whatever we ask in His Name will be granted to us. There are several instances where Jesus talked about this:

> *"And I will do [I Myself will grant] whatever you ask*
> *in My Name [as presenting all that I AM], so that the*
> *Father may be glorified and extolled in (through) the Son."*
> *[Yes] I will grant [I Myself will do for you] whatever you*
> *shall ask in My Name [as presenting all that I AM]."*
> *John 14:13-14*

He also talks about this in *John 15:16* and *John 16:23*. So you see the importance of this.

Don't get so caught up in legalism in saying "In Jesus Name" after everything you pray. You already have authority. You need to meditate on who you are in Christ and know your authority. Just because you may have not said "In Jesus Name" at the end of one of your prayers, doesn't mean it won't come to pass. All authority has been given to you by believing in Jesus Christ.

Praise Instead Of Petition

Praise is very important to God. He wants us to have a thankful, grateful heart. He enjoys that when we thank Him instead of complaining and asking Him for things all the time. Think of it this way. How do you like it when your kids are not thankful for what you give them? If all they did was ask you for things and never said thank you, you would not be excited to give them anything. Of course God loves us unconditionally, but we need to be careful that our asking doesn't outweigh our praise. *In Psalm 138:1-2, David said this: "I will confess and praise You [O God] with my whole heart; before the gods* will I sing praises to You. I will worship toward Your holy temple and praise Your name for Your loving-kindness and for Your truth and faithfulness; for You have exalted above all else Your name and Your word and You have magnified Your word above all Your name!"

When you pray your prayer, believe you receive the answer when you pray (*Mark 11:22-24*). Thank God that He has heard your prayer (*Psalm 66:19-20*) and thank Him by faith for the answer to your prayer. That will show the Father your trust and faith in Him. You believe that your prayer is already answered in the spiritual realm. You have not seen the manifestation of that prayer but you know that God is faithful. God likes that kind of faith.

We need to not be afraid to show our thankfulness to God around others. There are many people who are very religious and they do not like churches where people raise or clap their hands (*Psalm 47:1*) or where loud music is played. People talk real low if they are talking about God. *Psalm 63:3-4* says, "*Because Your loving-kindness is better than life, my lips shall praise You. So will I bless You while I live; I will lift up my hands in Your name.*"

We should be singing praises every day for everything God has done and is doing for us. *Psalm 126:2-3* says, "*Then were our mouths filled with laughter, and our tongues with singing. Then they said among the nations, The Lord has done great things for them. The Lord has done great things for us! We are glad!*"

These are just a few scriptures on what God has to say about praise and worship. You can see that God likes our praise and He wants us to sing and laugh. I remember as a kid, no one ever laughed in church. No one talked to anyone when you were sitting in the pew and we would look straight forward and not move. What kind of worship is that? Christianity is fun and not boring. We cannot be stiff necked and quiet. We live in the United States of America, a nation that was founded on Christianity. We should be praising God and talking about Him all the time. Instead, it has come to a point where there are places we should not speak about God in case we offend someone. Too bad if they are offended. God likes boldness and we should not be embarrassed because of what God has done for us. This is another topic in itself but I couldn't resist.

Be bold. Raise your hands. Give thanks to the Lord. Sing. Don't always ask Him for things. Most of your prayer time should be thanking and praising Him. There should be very little petition (requests). He has already provided us with everything we need. *Philippians 4:6* says this:

> *"Do not fret or have any anxiety about anything,*
> *but in every circumstance and in everything, by prayer*
> *and petition (definite requests), **with thanksgiving**,*
> *continue to make your wants known to God."*

God wants to be involved in everything you do. Continue to make your wants known to God but make praise a bigger part of your life. Praise Him throughout the day for everything.

Worship

Worship is not only for the church service, it is for anytime. It is for "all time". Worship Him at home. Kneel down and praise Him. Take communion at home. *Psalm 95:6* says, *"O come, let us worship and bow down, let us kneel before the Lord our Maker [in reverent praise and supplication]."* The word 'worship' means to love someone deeply, to treat someone as divine, and to show respect to. The word worship is first used in *Genesis 22:5* when Abraham was taking his son Isaac and offering him to God as a burnt offering. This was an act of obedience to God, a sacrifice.

To me worship is surrender and a sacrifice. It is an act of devotion. We are showing our love to God the Father and surrendering our life to Him. When we worship God, we are surrendering ourselves to Him and His ways. It is a surrender of everything-especially your mind. Because when you renew your mind to God's way of thinking, you will find out the will of God (*Romans 12:1-2*). You worship God because He loves you so much and chose you as His child. His way of living and doing things are so awesome and bring you such blessings and joy. You want to show your love to Him by meditating on His goodness.

We can worship Him with our finances. We are giving something that we see as valuable and doing what God asks us to do. We trust His Word knowing that He will pour out a blessing so big that we cannot contain it (*Malachi 3:10*).

When we worship God in church and when the music is being played and songs are being sung, we want to make that worship pleasing to God. It is not about what you get out of it. You show your devotion to Him and you reverence Him. You put Him above anything else that is in your life. You are lifting your hands and meditating on His goodness and love for you. I could go on and on but that is what worship is to me. We need to thank Him for everything He has already given us and will continue to do. But we need to just thank Him for Who He is, and not only for what He gives us.

Do not only thank God for the good things He does for you, but also praise Him in the wilderness. A mature Christian is not moved by trials and tribulations. God does not make bad things happen to us, but we live in a fallen world and things don't go perfectly. I look at trials as a way to develop and it gives God an opportunity to show His amazing power. When a trial comes your way, thank God that He loves you that much to give you a chance to develop and become all that He wants you to be. We will talk about this in the next chapter. When opposition comes, pray and believe your prayer is answered. God always causes us to triumph (*II Corinthians 2:14*). How can you not worship the Lord when you know that through every problem you will have victory? The devil will not know what to do with you when you stay happy during your trials. Worship is spiritual warfare. We need more worship, praise, and thanksgiving and less complaining and ungratefulness.

"All the earth shall bow down to You and sing
[praises] to You; they shall praise Your name in
song. Selah [pause, and calmly think of that]!
Psalm 66:4

Chapter 7

Developing Christian Character

God wants to show up and show out in these last days. He wants to use Christians as an advertisement of His goodness and power. Christians must renew their mind to the Truth of who they are in Christ and what they have inherited. Believers need to stand out. We are set apart for His use. We are a peculiar people-we are unique and belong to Him.

We need to develop Christian character. The word 'character' means the set of qualities that make someone distinctive. We should not blend in with the world. Christians should be the most loving, giving, healthiest, richest, and powerful people on the earth. But most of the Christians I know and meet do not stand out. They talk and think like the people in the world.

I often hear people say things like, "God put this sickness on me to teach me a lesson". "God is making me go through this to punish me." Just take a moment and think about how ridiculous that sounds. God is a loving god and does not put sickness or calamity on His people. Who would want a relationship with someone like that? I wouldn't. "God caused that earthquake to teach that country a lesson". This kind of talk and belief needs to stop. The Old Covenant has been replaced with the New Covenant of grace. God's not pouring out His wrath on people because of their sins. Sin has been dealt with through Jesus Christ. God is not looking at your sins. He will not judge you because of your sins but whether you believed in His Son (*John 16:8-11*).

In the Old Covenant, God's blessings were based on their performance. When they sinned, they needed to make an animal sacrifice, their sins were forgiven until the next time they sinned. They were blessed because of their sacrifice (*Exodus 20:24*). But in the New Covenant of grace, Jesus became sin for us (*II Corinthians 5:21*) and took our sickness and poverty. He was the perfect sacrifice for us. We are blessed because of His sacrifice. God does not put sickness on people nor cause them to go through things to punish them. Jesus took your sickness and all punishment on Himself at Calvary. Sin, sickness, and poverty are His, not yours.

There has been so much wrong teaching and it has been carried down through generations. But I also believe it is a way to put blame on someone else other than ourselves. People don't want to take responsibility for anything. When people go through trials, they pray to God to get them out of it. God does not put bad things on His children, but we live in a fallen world and bad things are going to happen. Jesus put it this way in *John 16:33*:

> *"I have told you these things, so that in Me you*
> *may have [perfect] peace and confidence. In the*
> *world you have tribulation and trials and distress*
> *and frustration; but be of good cheer [take courage;*
> *be confident, certain, undaunted]! For I have*
> *overcome the world. [I have deprived it of power*
> *to harm you <u>and have conquered it for you.</u>]"*

We will have trouble and if you are a Christian get ready because the devil knows your destiny and he will try to attack you with all kinds of things. What do I say to this? I say, "Devil, hit me with your best shot, you are a defeated foe. God is on my side and if God be for me, who can be against me" (*Romans 8:31*)? When you have this kind of attitude, the devil does not know what to do with you. Learning how to stay calm through the storms of your life is key to a victorious life. If Jesus says to cheer up, then we can do that. You need to know that God loves you and that He has a good plan for your life (*Jeremiah*

29:11). You need to renew your mind to God's Word to find out all the promises of God and to know what to do and say when those storms come.

One thing I want to mention, and I have touched on this a little, is that people get the Old and New Testament mixed up. They are mixing the Law of the Old Covenant and the New Covenant of grace. Read *Galatians 4.* Verse five says that Jesus redeemed us from the Law. Verse four says that Jesus was born of a woman and born subject to the Law. Jesus preached the Law in the Gospels. You have to be able to divide the Word and learn from the Holy Spirit when Jesus is teaching Law and when He is teaching the New Covenant that was to come after His death and resurrection. The New Testament actually did not start until Jesus died. There had to be a death in order for the New Covenant to come into place *(Hebrews 9:12-18).* After Jesus' death, the New Covenant came into place and the Law had been established for the Jewish people to be justified and declared righteous with God *(Galatians 3:24).* The Law came into effect during Moses' time. The New Covenant of grace is for <u>Jews and Gentiles</u> (Gentiles were those that were not under the Law). *Galatians 3:28* says, *"There is [now no distinction] neither Jew nor Greek, there is neither slave nor free, there is not male and female; <u>for you are all one in Christ Jesus.</u>"* Now we are righteous when we believe in Jesus Christ and we receive all that He died for us to have *(II Corinthians 5:21 & Romans 5:19).* Quit trying to earn God's blessings by your performance and find out what you have inherited through grace. God sees you as righteous as Jesus and He's not looking at what you do wrong or right.

Someone might say, "You mean we don't have to follow the Ten Commandments?" As a New Covenant believer in Jesus Christ, you are righteous and the Law is not for the righteous *(I Timothy 1:9).* When you follow Christ, you live by the Spirit, not the Law. Sin, for example stealing from someone, will not send you to hell if you've been born again and truly believe in your heart in Jesus Christ. The only sin that will send you to hell is not believing in Jesus *(John 16:8-9).* Once you get that, you won't look at people and their sin. If you met a murderer on the street, but He was born again and had turned his life over to Christ, you wouldn't look at him and think, "Wow, this guy murdered someone, he's going to hell". No, not if he believes in Jesus. The religious people are the ones that look down their holy nose and judge people for what they've done wrong. This stinks in the nostrils of God. That self-righteous attitude is not right. And it is giving Christianity a bad rap.

The Holy Spirit will lead and guide you. If you are attentive to His voice, He will say, "It's not good to lie or murder". I'm putting this mildly and plainly. When you follow Christ, He will lead you. You will make mistakes but God still loves you. But as you mature with the Lord, you will change. You may have lied to people most of your life, but if you are seeking God and renewing your mind to His Word, you will begin to know that lying is wrong. Change comes, and little by little your character will resemble the character of Christ. But you need to work at it. We don't do everything perfect to get God to love us. He already loves us unconditionally when we receive Jesus as our Savior and Lord. It is impossible to keep all the ten and that is why God made a New Way.

I am not a Jewish scholar and by no means understand how God is so merciful with us when we believe in Jesus. Following Him is the greatest, most enjoyable thing you can do. Once you understand the difference of the Old Covenant and the New, everything will make sense. You can begin to live a life that is so awesome. I try to make this as simple as I can. I may not get everything exactly right but I think I come close.

That's why love is the greatest commandment. We have to know who we are in Christ and know we are righteous. We need to love one another as Christ loves us. Jesus is our perfect example of love. Learn about how we live in the New Covenant and get rid of those awful, religious beliefs. We need to show people the love of God, then they will want to know Him. When we are mixing the Old and New, we are destroying what God had intended to be so beautiful.

Plain and simple-Jesus is the only Way to heaven and the only way to the Father. We can live heaven on earth and be free of the power of sin, poverty, sickness, and oppression from the enemy. God wants us to have everything that they have in heaven and he wants us to have it here on earth. We don't need those things in heaven because they already exist. He wants us to live heaven on earth so when we die, we won't even know we died. We just go from glory to the next glory. We have inherited everything I mentioned **now**! The end of *II Corinthians 6:2* says, *"...**now** is the day of salvation."* Is that sweet? Receive your inheritance and be free today!!

You don't have to live under bondage. *Galatians 4:7(NIV)* says, *"So you are no longer a slave, but a son; and since you are a son, God has made you also an heir."* Read the Bible for yourself. Can it get any plainer? You don't have to wear your skirt to the floor and be afraid to wear makeup. I thank God for makeup! You don't have to be restricted to certain foods or keep certain laws and rituals. Look again at *Galatians 3:28*. Jewish people don't have to live like they do. You are justified and made right with God through Jesus Christ. **He is the Messiah**. The Messiah has already come! You people are deceived and you know who you are. I am saying this in love and am saddened by all the different religions and the rules that go along with them. No wonder people don't want to follow God. They think they have to follow all the rules of a religion and do everything right. There are many people that are good people that are following a certain religion, but they are under bondage. I'm not picking on any one denomination or religion. Find out the Truth of God's Word and you will be set free to enjoy your life and be a witness to others of God's goodness. God loves you unconditionally and He doesn't love you based on your performance.

Deal With Your Stuff

As I talked about above, trials will happen and how we react to those problems is crucial. Our first reaction will set the stage on how things will go. If we fall apart right away when something bad happens, there is a reason. Number one is that you may not know what God promises you in His Word and number two may be that you are not rooted and grounded in the love of God. Most people think God is there to deliver them out of all their problems. God is here to help us but He also loves us too much to allow us to stay where we are at. If you never encouraged your child to walk and was satisfied with him or her just crawling around, your child would never develop the strength in his or her legs. We will go through things and this gives you a chance to develop patience.

Our character as a Christian is a result of the pressure that is put on us. When we find out what God's promises are, we know that we win in every arena of life. When we find out God's way of overcoming trials, we become stronger and stronger and are a huge witness to others around us. When we are strong through our trials because we are trusting God and doing things His way, people will see that we are Christians because of certain characteristics that we have. We have a certain quality about us that we are not moved by our circumstances and always see everything in the positive because we know that God always causes us to triumph and He is always with us. *Romans 15:4* says that by our steadfast and patient endurance and the encouragement drawn from the Scriptures we might hold fast to and cherish hope. Faith and patience come by knowing that God loves you and His Word is true. You already have the victory through Him. He always comes through no matter what. It may not be in your timing but He is faithful. If what you are hoping for has not yet come to pass, keep believing God because He is faithful and you will bear much fruit (*Psalms 1:3 & John 15:5*).

A third thing that affects how we react to problems is not dealing with root issues in our life. You cannot develop and grow in loving others if you do not love yourself. You cannot be forgiving toward other people if you don't forgive someone in your past for abusing you. There is always a reason why people do the things they do. And if we keep covering up that problem by running to the doctor and taking a pill to ease the pain or we depend on alcohol to cover up our past, we will never get to the root of the problem and it will be a cycle that repeats itself. Issues in your life have to be dealt with. By allowing the Holy Spirit to help you see what you need to work on, you can grow into all that God has for you.

If you have trouble receiving from God, God is never the problem. He has already provided everything. It is our receiving that is the problem. This is a heart issue. There is some belief or hurt deep down in your heart that is hindering you from receiving all that God has for you. Jesus said in the end of *Matthew 12:34, "...For out of the fullness (the overflow, the superabundance) of the heart the mouth speaks."* Whatever is in your heart will come out of your mouth. If you believe that God doesn't love you and you feel bad for something you've done in your past, that will hinder you from receiving. Not receiving is always a heart issue. See yourself forgiven, healed, delivered, and prosperous. People need to dig deep and work with the Holy Spirit so they can get rid of all the junk that is hidden deep down inside of them. There may be religious beliefs that are keeping you in bondage. Remember that we are not under bondage any more but you are a son or daughter of God and heirs of His promise.

People will say to me, "I wish I had a relationship with God like you do. I wish I could read the Bible and understand it." I did not get it wishing and I am nobody special that I hear from God more than the next person. *"Come close to God and He will come close to you"(James 4:8).* It can't get any plainer. You must seek God. He wants to have a deep, intimate relationship with you. He's available all the time.

By being baptized in the Holy Spirit, you will have all that God has for you. Understanding the Bible will be easier and will be taught to you by the Holy Spirit. He will reveal to you what you need to work on. But you must seek God and make spending time with Him a priority. If you want to get to know someone, you must spend time with them. We cannot see Jesus in the flesh , but we can spend time with Him by talking to Him and by reading His Word. The Holy Spirit was sent to us so we could know Jesus and God the Father and make them known to the world. We also must get quiet and listen to what He is saying to us. *"Be still and know that I am God..." (Psalm 46:10).*

Getting quiet today is more difficult because of all the technology we have-computer, TV with hundreds of channels, cell phones, etc. Take time to be quiet and turn everything off. And pay attention to other people. <u>Learn to listen</u>. I know countless amounts of people who talk constantly. They only talk about themselves. You cannot hear from God when you talk all the time. And please have a two-way conversation and show interest in the other person. I may be touching on another subject here but it is a sore spot with me and a big problem. Ask questions and find out about the other person. Care about other people instead of always thinking about yourself. Let someone talk without always bringing the conversation back on you. Don't get me started on this. This is selfish and a huge problem in society. *Proverbs 18:2* says, *"A [self-confident] fool has no delight in understanding but only in revealing his personal opinions and himself."* Now back to the subject at hand.

God is the One who attracts and draws us and gives us the desire to want a relationship with Jesus. He does this through the ministry of the Holy Spirit.

> *"No one is able to come to Me unless the Father*
> *Who sent Me attracts and draws him and gives*
> *him the desire to come to Me, and [then] I will*
> *raise him up [from the dead] at the last day."*
> *John 6:44*

The Holy Spirit is the one who will lead you. I did not wake up one day and say I was going to seek God. The Holy Spirit got a hold of me and revealed Himself to me.

I began to not like doing certain things. I didn't know what was going on at the time but God the Father was drawing me in. The Holy Spirit was correcting me (*Hebrews 12:8-11*) and showing me a better way to live so that I could come up higher. He had something better for me than the way I was living. I was obedient to the Holy Spirit's leading. I remember being in Texas and the television set where I was staying was always on this one channel in the morning. The program was led by a woman named Joyce Meyer. God directed my steps and I was interested in what she had to say.

I started watching her program every day. Joyce is a great Bible teacher and came from an abusive background. I would hear her talking about something that I knew I had a problem with. One of the first things God dealt with me about was worry. I grew up around people who worried. If Joyce was talking about how she used to worry, I would write down the scriptures she mentioned and then study them on my own. I would memorize them and confess them out loud like she said. The Holy Spirit would lead me to other scriptures as well.

Once you become a Christian, you are not your own (*I Corinthians 6:19*). God has so many promises that He has already provided. If we are worrying, we are not trusting God. When a situation came up where I was tempted to worry, the Holy Spirit would remind me of what God's Word says and I would immediately be released of being tempted to worry. He would either bring the scripture to my remembrance or I would look it up and read it. It is best to always go to the Word instead of depending on them by memory (*Joshua 1:8 & Proverbs 4:20-21*). Instead of worry, I chose to trust God and meditate on His Word. I was obedient to the Holy Spirit's leading. The Holy Spirit is always dealing with many people but many are not listening.

As I said before, I think most people want God to deliver them out of things. I listen to how people pray and most prayers are asking God for a way out of their trial. We need to do our part. Most people have past issues that need to be dealt with. They cannot be swept under the rug.

People I know do not say, "Boy, God is sure dealing with me about being selfish." I don't know if I've ever heard anyone say that besides a preacher or me. God deals with me about stuff constantly. There is layer upon layer of things He deals with me about. I am glad of it and have grown so much. I keep a journal and write down the things God has me work on. I also write down the victories I have experienced as I work through each area. This is the only way we will develop. We need to find out what God's Word says to do.

Judging other people is not good. What right do I have to judge people for what they do or don't do? I don't have to give an account for their lives when I get to heaven. I only need to answer for my life. Everyone is at a different level in their walk with God. Most of the problem is that they have been taught the wrong thing. People need to find out the Truth of God's Word. The greatest commandment, Jesus said, is to love one another as He has loved us (*John 15:12*). If you know that love always believes the best (*I Corinthians 13:7*), then you know judgment is wrong. Love covers and judgment exposes. I had a problem in this area. I have not fully conquered everything but I am growing. Progress is key.

Again, dealing with issues from your past and/or present is one of the first steps a person should take. Allow the Holy Spirit to reveal to you what you need to work on. People can hold on to things and act as if their life is perfect, but that root will fester inside of you. Things will always surface somewhere. By and large, things will surface through your physical body. *Proverbs 14:30* says, *"A calm and undisturbed mind and heart are the life and health of the body, but envy, jealousy, and wrath are like rottenness of the bones."*

Many diseases are a result of people's anger they have toward someone who has mistreated them. When you rid yourself of all the junk that you are harboring, you can move forward into what God has for you. You will be able to help other people and your health will improve. I know people who are in bad shape physically and they may deny that they carry any anger or jealousy toward someone in their life. I know that is a cover up. Some things can be buried so deep inside it takes a while to surface. Others want to deny the whole thing and think it doesn't matter. These things will come out in your health. Buried feelings will also affect your relationships. Your past has to be dealt with and by cleaning out your closet so to speak, you will be on your way to a joyful, healthy life.

Hardships do workout your character. My main goal in this chapter is for you to realize that actual trials will make you better in every way if you follow God's way. By doing things God's way, you can grow in many ways in which you have more and more patience toward situations and people because you know God is faithful. But if you are holding on to things from your past or are in strife with someone today, that is going to affect how you handle things in life. We feed our physical body food for strength. We need to feed our spirit the Word of God. The power that comes from feeding your spirit the Word of God is faith. When you have faith in every area and know that God always provides a way out of every trial and everything that comes against you (*I Corinthians 10:13*), you will become stronger and stronger spiritually and receive all the spiritual blessings He has provided and walk in victory in every step you take. Your character will develop and that is when people will take notice and want what you have. A relationship with our Lord is for anyone who will come to Him. Much effort is involved and there is an exchange that must take place. You must do your part and become a witness to others so that others will want a relationship with Jesus. God wants us to have a victorious life.

James 1:12 says, *"Blessed (happy, to be envied) is the man who is patient under trial and stands up under temptation, for when he has stood the test and been approved, he will receive [the victor's] crown of life which God has promised to those who love Him."* We are blessed and to be envied when we go through trials and keep a good attitude because we know God loves us. We can stay patient because we ask for God's help and He leads us and guides us and even if things don't look good in the natural, we know God always causes us to triumph. We remain patient during trials and people will want to know Jesus.

We cannot just accept Jesus as the One Who forgives our sins and then expect Him to do everything for us after that. We must feed our spirit and become all that He wants us to be. We need to renew our mind to the Word of God. We must be vitally connected to Jesus and sow His Word in our heart, then we can ask whatever we will and He shall do it (*John 15:7*). What a great exchange He offers us.

Dealing with the issues in your life will help you develop in every way. The way you deal with your issues is by spending time with the Holy Spirit and let Him reveal His Truth to you. Allow Him to be your Helper and Comforter (*John 14:26*). Take from Him and become all He wants you to be.

Development Through Pressure

Everyone wants to run away from their troubles and wants to get out of situations with ease. But by going through trials and trusting in God and doing things His way, your life becomes better and you will be able to help someone else that is experiencing the same thing you went through. Your Christian character is developed by the pressures you encounter.

You will not develop muscles by not lifting weights. Pressure must be applied and that muscle needs to be torn down in order to build up stronger. In life, we will be torn down as well but we don't have to stay down. When you are rooted and grounded in the love of God and know His Word, you will have the armor you need to combat any situation you face.

The Word of God is our armor to stand against anything the enemy possesses (*Ephesians 6:13*). Pressure is applied on your life through trials. If you don't have any problems, you will not develop into what God wants you to be. You renew your mind to the Word of God and meditate on His Truths. You confess what God's Word says instead of talking about your problem. Your faith will rise when you speak what God says (*Romans 10:17*). If you don't know this, you will just cry out to God to help you.

When knowing the Word, you can confess His Truth and know that you are covered. A problem will arise and you stand strong on the Word. You praise God that He always causes you to triumph (*II Corinthians 2:14*). You trust God and are at peace. Your trust will develop and when another storm comes along, you will be stronger each time. You become stronger in your physical body when you continue to work out and your muscles develop. You will become strong spiritually when you spend time in the Word. When the storms of life come, you are not even moved because you are rooted in the Word of God

If you don't know His Word, you are like a person in an ocean without a life preserver. You won't have peace if you don't know the Giver of Peace. You cannot have peace during a storm if you don't know what God says to do during it. You will go down in your emotions and sink and allow the devil to win every time. God has given us His Word so we know what to do when those storms come. We need to develop as Christians and become tougher and tougher with each difficulty.

When you are mature in your faith, you will actually not bat an eye at problems. You can get to a point that you can even laugh. You may say, "You're crazy". Why? God has said in His Word that we are more than conquerors *(Romans 8:37)*. That means that we have the victory before we even have the problem. If you don't think you can do that then you are looking at your situation in the natural and thinking that you have to get yourself out of it. You are not believing and trusting God.

Jesus said in *John 14:1, "Do not let your hearts be troubled (distressed, agitated). You believe in and adhere to and trust in and rely on God; believe in and adhere to and trust in and rely also on Me."* He was about to go to the cross and He told His disciples not to be troubled. If Jesus says we should not be troubled, we can do it. We cannot look at our situations in the natural. We must look at the supernatural realm. We must look to what we cannot see because what we can see is temporary and what we cannot see is eternal *(II Corinthians 4:18)*. What we can see in the natural is subject to change. But God's Word is eternal and the Word of God is called incorruptible Seed *(I Peter 1:23)*. This means that God's Word will always produce. It cannot fail. There may be no way in the natural that you can see a way out of your problem, but Jesus said to not be troubled and to believe in God. We spend way too much time looking at things the way they appear and not enough time looking at the supernatural realm and what God has already done and what He is able to do. *Blessed are those who believe and have never seen (John 20:29)*.

Give the devil a nervous breakdown by thanking God that He has delivered you from your problem from the start. Praise the Lord that He loves you that much for you to develop. Your setback allows God an opportunity to show His amazing power. The enemy does not know what to do with a person of faith that reacts like this.

My husband's car got stolen once and when he called me I was a little upset but I immediately went to the Word and stood on what God says. I actually was laughing and glad that God would have an opportunity to show His amazing power. We both stood on the Word and remained at peace. The next day the car was found without even a scratch. The thief didn't even take the change that was in the car. *Malachi 3:10-11* says that when we bring our tithes to God, He will rebuke the devourer (the thief in our case) for our sake. That is exactly what He did. I think the person that took the car got so afraid that they didn't have time to do any damage. God's hand was upon us protecting our property. He will always come through. We must develop through the pressures of life. But we will not know what God has done for us if we don't renew our mind to His Word.

Take The Challenge and Change

Many times it is not only our situations that we want to change, we also want the people in our life to change as well. We ask God to please change our spouse, our kids, or our co-workers. Granted, there are times when someone may be doing something that is hurting them and may need to be confronted. But there are times when God is wanting us to change.

So many people run away from their development. I did that many times in a job or in relationships. If things got tough, I jumped ship. I didn't realize that if I had kept certain people in my life, I could have had an amazing friendship or that relationship would have helped me to change and become better. But I didn't have a relationship with God at that time and didn't know any better. It was all about me. I've heard it said this way, "It isn't how someone is treating you, it is how you are treating them." It doesn't matter how someone is treating you. We as Christians have to do what is right and love when we don't feel like it. Do you think Jesus felt like going to the cross? Love is not a feeling, it is an action. Christ did that for us as an act of love.

There are things we must do that we don't feel like doing. But if we will change instead of changing that other person, we will become better. Are you willing to go through some hard times in order to help someone else? By being merciful to someone and loving them, they will see your strength and then all of a sudden they change. You both grow in the relationship.

I believe God created family for us to develop. Without a spouse or mother-in-law (and I love my mother-in-law), we would never develop into what God wants us to be. I believe this is the area where we grow the most. There are many families that are broken up because of petty disagreements. People are so stubborn and want to be right. You don't always have to get your way. Who cares if your family member gets more of an inheritance than you? God is your supplier. Let someone else have something without you squabbling about it.

The devil loves it when spouses and families are at strife. He wants you to be offended. When you are offended, you lose your power and anointing. We've got to do what God wants us to do. We have to love one another as Jesus loves us. There is so much strife and offense among Christians. They act no different than the people of the world. We need to stand out. We need to forgive when someone has stolen from us or bad mouthed us. Quit being so touchy and sensitive about what someone is doing to you or not doing for you. Get your eyes off of yourself and help others no matter what. Don't let the enemy have an inroad in your life. It is total freedom when you don't pay attention when someone has wronged you or treated you bad. They don't know any better or are having a bad day. Maybe they have their mind on something important and just didn't realize what they were doing to you. Whatever the case may be, don't allow other people to affect how you live your life. Love people and don't take the devil's bait of offense.

Whatever you make happen for someone else, God will make happen for you. Get over yourself and let God fight your battles. Let God be your Vindicator (*Psalm 135:14*). If someone has done something to you, keep loving that person. God will deal with them.

You do what is right and God will do the rest. Love people and treat them well despite the way they are treating you.

> *"Do nothing from factional motives [through contentiousness, strife, selfishness, or for unworthy ends] or prompted by conceit and empty arrogance. Instead, in the true spirit of humility (lowliness of mind) let each regard the others as better than and superior to himself [thinking more highly of one another than you do of yourselves]. Let each of you esteem and look upon and be concerned for not [merely] his own interests, but also each for the interests of others. Let this same attitude and purpose and [humble] mind be in you which was in Christ Jesus: [Let Him be your example in humility:]"*
> *Philippians 2:3-5*

Once you know who you are in Christ, you will not be bothered if someone mistreats you. Overcome evil with good (*Romans 12:21*). Train yourself to look at people's positive points. Don't always focus on what people are not. People are so touchy and get hurt if someone is rude to them or they are mistreated. Quit having such high expectations of other people. We are all different and not everyone will do what you want them to do. We have to come up higher and not get offended. Consider the other person's life. There are things you do not know about them. In order to develop Christian character, we need to learn how Jesus treated people. We need to study His ways of loving and doing things. In *John 13:34*, Jesus said, *"I give you a new commandment: that you should love one another. Just as I have loved you, so you too should love one another."*

When we focus on what others are doing to us or have done to us, we are selfish. We are looking inward when we need to look to Jesus. He has done everything. He has given us a way to live that goes against the way the world reacts. We are to bless those that hurt us. It is the devil's intention to get us to always look at what is wrong or to look at how something is affecting us or focusing on how we feel. Don't go by how you feel or what the doctor says, go by what the Word says. If we take the cares and distractions of this world upon ourselves, we choke the Word. The Word cannot perform when we are consumed with self. Jesus said this in *Mark 4:17-20*. He said don't be offended and don't let those cares creep in because the Word becomes fruitless. We won't reap the 30, 60 and 100 fold return. Keep your eyes on Jesus and what He has already done and His way of doing things.

There has never been another human being who was more mistreated than Jesus Christ, yet He kept a good attitude. He did what He was called to do and He did it for all of us. I believe we can take the challenge and change. Practice being good to people when they are mistreating you. We need to show Jesus to the world and the way we do that is by loving people who may not deserve it. When a person comes into your life and they rub you like sandpaper, study love and come up higher. Instead of getting that person out of your life, take the challenge and change. You will become stronger and be able to deal with many different personalities.

In the first part of *Philippians 3:10* the apostle Paul said, *"My determined purpose is that I may know Him [that I may progressively become more deeply and intimately acquainted with Him, perceiving and recognizing and understanding the wonders of His Person more strongly and more clearly], and that I may in that same way come to know the power outflowing from His resurrection...".* We need to be determined to know Jesus like that. In the Old Testament people were conscious of their sin, but we are now in the New Covenant and we need to be conscious of only Jesus. We need to be studying His character and how He treated people. When we do that, we will make an impact on this world and people will also want a relationship with our Wonderful Lord.

Trials Develop Character

Going through hard times is the only way you can develop in life. To see God come through as His Word says, you will have to go through things. If we never had any problems we wouldn't need any faith. If everything were easy we wouldn't need God. We must develop our character and become like Jesus.

As I said earlier, 'character' is defined as a set of qualities that make someone distinctive. When you are born again, your spirit is brand new (*II Corinthians 5:17*). You must renew your mind to the Word of God so that your spirit will dominate over your body and soul. When we renew our mind, we will find out how we are to act in response to trials. People will see that you have a certain quality about you. You are stable no matter what happens. This is what the apostle Paul said in *Romans 5:3-4*:

> *"Moreover [let us also be full of joy now!] let us*
> *exult and triumph in our troubles and rejoice in our*
> *sufferings, knowing that pressure and affliction and*
> *hardship produce patient and unswerving endurance.*
> *And endurance (fortitude) develops maturity of*
> *character (approved faith and tried integrity).*
> *And character [of this sort] produces [the habit of]*
> *joyful and confident hope of eternal salvation."*

Notice he says to rejoice in our sufferings. When I first read that, it was astounding. Through each hardship we go through we will become stronger and stronger. The Amplified version says hardship produces patience and endurance. First of all, the King James Version doesn't use the word produce, it uses the word workout. There is a big difference. If hardships produced endurance then everyone would be in victory. But that is not so. Tough times **workout** endurance.

This is similar to exercise. We don't produce muscles just because we watch an exercise tape. We must physically do the work in order for those muscles to develop. We must do many repetitions and after substantial time, the muscles become larger. When you renew your mind to the Word of God you will see His promises. You trust Him and depend on Him. By going through a hard time we find out that God always causes us to triumph. He will never allow more to come on us than we can bear and He will always provide a way out. We see His faithfulness and the next time a problem arises we are not even shaken over it because of the triumph we saw last time. We become more patient and are able to endure more. Our faith and patience will develop because God has always come through and He will come through again.

Endurance is the ability to go further and further, the ability to withstand whatever comes. After each trial, we will be able to take more and more until soon each thing that happens to us will not phase us. We know that God is faithful and our character will depict **His** power and victory not our own strength.

The problem many people have is trying to do everything in their own strength. They do not rely on the Holy Spirit at all. They pray futile prayers with no power whatsoever. I will preach the baptism in the Holy Spirit until Jesus comes back. You will not have any power until you receive the baptism in the Holy Spirit with the evidence of speaking in tongues. You cannot grow through trials without the help of the Strengthener (Holy Spirit). Praying in tongues is a must everyday but especially through trials. Your mind may not know how to pray during the challenge you are having but when you pray in the spirit, the Holy Spirit prays the perfect prayer (*Romans 8:26-27*). Praying in tongues will edify you and you will be built up (*I Corinthians 14:4*). Nothing bothers you, not because you are a super saint, but because you depend on the Holy Spirit for everything.

Do Good And Remain Strong Under Pressure

Again, you cannot do this in your own strength. Another name for the Holy Spirit is Helper. Allow Him to lead and guide you into what you need to do. He will teach you all things. Listen to Him and allow Him to change you.

Our flesh is lazy and wants its own way. It would be easier to cast someone out of your life instead of loving them when they don't deserve it. We don't deserve God's love but He loves us no matter what. By casting people out of our life we will never make an impact in this world for Jesus. We have to do things we've never done to get things we've never had. You may work with someone who is hard to get along with. They are moody and rude and rub you the wrong way. You could find another job but maybe you are called to stay in that position to come up higher yourself and also change their life. That woman at work that is always moody may have a husband who is beating her or verbally abusing her. There may be things in this woman's past that make her the way she is. She has never been treated right by anyone in her whole family. If you do what is right and love her, you will not only change her life but will grow yourself. What a great deal. Instead of only thinking about yourself and how that woman is affecting you, you put yourself aside and love when you don't feel like it. You do it to help her. You will become more like Jesus and will develop patience with others that have various personalities. *James 1:2-4* in the Message translation says it like this:

> *Consider it a sheer gift, friends, when tests and*
> *challenges come at you from all sides. You know that*
> *under pressure, your faith-life is forced into the open*
> *and shows its true colors. So don't try to get out of*
> *anything prematurely. Let it do its work so you become*
> *mature and well-developed, not deficient in any way.*

I like how this translation puts it. Don't try to get out of anything prematurely. Let it do its work so you become mature and well-developed, not deficient in any way. That is great. If you were to quit your job prematurely just because this woman is being a pain, you wouldn't develop and that woman may never get saved or run across anyone who shows her the love of Jesus. You may be her only connection to Jesus. Both of your lives will be impacted in a positive way. Then you and this woman can go forth stronger and future relationships will be impacted by the love of Christ.

Be Careful What You Say

What you say during trials is very important. You may have to share your situation with someone but don't keep talking about it.

God will get tired of hearing about it as well as family or co-workers. The power of life and death is in the tongue (*Proverbs 18:21*). When you are in a trial or come across someone who is hard to get along with, ask the Holy Spirit what to do. Pray and ask Him to change you and to help you know what to do. Pray for opportunities to show the love of Jesus to that person. Study love and mercy. We need to go to the One Who knows what to do. We need to seek the One Who is our Helper and Teacher.

Pray and believe that that person or situation has changed. Confess victory, not the problem. If Mary at work is difficult to get along with, pray and ask God to help you to know what to do. Bind that spirit of selfishness off of her. Pray that she would have a desire to know the Lord and to use you. Confess that Mary is a loving and kind co-worker. Then keep doing what is right and pretty soon Mary will change. The bonus is that you've changed as well.

The first part of *Psalm 37:3* says this: *Trust (lean on, rely on, and be confident) in the Lord and do good...*" Quit talking about the problem and do what God says to do.

I talked about this in Chapter five. Jesus said in *Matthew 6:31,* *"Therefore take no thought, saying...".* You may get thoughts in your head that aren't good but you need to think on what is good as it talks about in *Philippians 4:8.* The minute you speak what you are thinking, you give it power. If it is negative, don't speak. You will get negative thoughts because the battle is in your mind. Cast down those thoughts and think on what the Word says. Speak God's end result, not the problem.

Show the love of Jesus when you don't feel like it. You **can** love someone when you don't feel like it. Jesus did not feel like going to the cross. He did it for us. When you have trials in your life, follow God's way and your character will develop as a Christian. Speak God's Word and not what is going on in your life. Then the people you come in contact with will see the love of Jesus and want to know the God you serve.

Chapter 8

Supernatural vs. Natural

"God is a Spirit (a spiritual Being) and those who worship Him must worship Him in spirit and in truth (reality)."
John 4:24

"Therefore if any person is [ingrafted] in Christ (the Messiah) he is a new creation (a new creature altogether); the old [previous moral and spiritual condition] has passed away. Behold, the fresh and new has come!
II Corinthians 5:17

"May blessing (praise, laudation, and eulogy) be to the God and Father of our Lord Jesus Christ (the Messiah) **Who has blessed us** *in Christ with every spiritual (given by the Holy Spirit) blessing in the heavenly realm!"*
Ephesians 1:3

When I was growing up, I remember people would say, "I won't believe it until I see it". If you look at that statement, it is really a tragedy. This is not at all the way the Kingdom of God works. In the Kingdom of God you must believe before you can see. People are born again and they receive Christ by faith. They cannot see Him in the flesh but confess that He is their Savior, that He died for their sins, and rose again from the dead, and believe that He lives on the inside of them. Why is that easy to believe without seeing, yet we have a hard time believing that we are healed physically or prosperous? Being born again involves our spirit which we cannot feel. But receiving healing and prosperity involves your five senses which tend to dominate in most cases. Your back hurts and you feel it. Your checkbook shows a negative balance and you see that and what you see and feel tends to dominate. We have to renew our mind to the Word of God so that what's in our spirit takes over the way we feel and what we see.

There are many things people will pray for and still talk like they really don't believe their prayer will even be answered. People are destroyed for lack of knowledge (*Hosea 4:6*). Many do not have any knowledge of the Truth and many do not read the Bible for themselves. People tend to live by their five senses. Therefore the natural world is more real to them than the supernatural things of God.

Many are living with one foot in the world and one toe in the Kingdom. I have heard someone say, "I'm praying like crazy. I pray and I worry". That is actually what I've heard people say. **That is not faith**. God said whenever you pray, believe you receive and you will have it. When you pray, you believe you receive <u>at that time</u>-- your prayer is answered at the time you pray. Study *Mark 11:22-24*. People are praying and trying to answer their own prayer. They are working and not allowing God to do His work. That's not living in the supernatural. That is not faith and it is not trusting God.

People asked Jesus what they were to do to carry out what God requires and He said *believe in the One Whom He has sent* (*John 6:28-29*). You will never receive from God when you're trying to do His job. He is saying, "Ok, you think you can do this? Knock yourself out". We have to relate more to the supernatural than the natural. There may be things that look so impossible but you have to believe that God is bigger than your situation or your sickness. You cannot go by what you see, hear, feel, taste, and smell. You must believe things like a little child. Someone raised from the dead after two days? I've heard accounts of this. If you say, "There is no way". You need to get your mind out of the way and go by what the Word says.

The word 'supernatural' in Webster's means departure from what is usual or normal. One of the definitions of the word 'natural' in Webster's is occurring in conformity with the ordinary course of nature, not marvelous or supernatural. Do you want a natural, ordinary life or do you want a supernatural life which is a life that is over and above? *Ephesians 3:20* says, *"Now to Him Who, by (in consequence of) the [action of His] power that is at work within us, is able to [carry out His purpose and] do superabundantly, far over and above all that we [dare] ask or think [infinitely beyond our highest prayers, desires, thoughts, hopes, or dreams]."*

We see numerous accounts of Jesus performing miracles--the dead raised, blind eyes opened, people healed of sickness, and the lame that walked. This is what we should be seeing today. I imagine these things happening today and know that one of the ways people will believe in Jesus Christ is by seeing these miracles. Jesus said we will see greater things. But we have come from a society where we have to see to believe. The supernatural is not talked about. When you hear the word supernatural many think of ghosts or magic. We live in a society of a hardened heart. We are hardened to the things of God and such miracles seem unreal or impossible.

God wants you to have a great life. He doesn't want you to just live an ordinary life but an extraordinary life. He wants you to be blessed in every area so you can be a blessing to others and a witness of His goodness. The only way we can have this over and above life is to learn to do what God says to do. In *Mark 4:24*, Jesus said this: *"Be careful what you are hearing. The measure [of thought and study] you give [to the truth you hear] will be the measure [of virtue and knowledge] that comes back to you--and more [besides] will be given to you who hear."*

If you do not study God's Word and get it into your heart, you will not have revelation knowledge of His promises and Truth. The more revelation knowledge you have of what God has done for you, the more power and peace you will have in your life. God has provided us with everything we need. We need to find out what He has provided and believe His Word over what our checkbook says or what the doctor says.

Most churches do not teach the full Gospel. They believe healing went away with the disciples. Read Jesus' prayer in *John 17:20*. Everything Jesus and the disciples did we are suppose to do also. It's right there in *John 17*. But if your church does not teach this, you will not have faith for this. Faith comes by hearing and the measure of truth and study you hear will be the measure of virtue and knowledge that comes back to you. The word virtue is dunamis power. This is the same power that created the heavens and the earth and the same power that raised Jesus from the dead. When you have the revelation knowledge of all God has for you and that you have the power of God through the Holy Spirit in you, nothing the devil throws at you will phase you. You will be able to tell that cancer to be gone in the Name of Jesus. You will know beyond a shadow of a doubt that God wants you well and prosperous and you will not let your mind talk you out of it. You will know that Jesus already paid the price for your healing and you're not trying to get healed, you <u>are</u> healed. We have to get to this point. This will take study of the Truth of God's Word and receive the Truth by faith.

For Jesus, it did not make sense in His mind that Lazarus could be raised from the dead after four days (*John 11*). He didn't let His mind get in the way. If you don't step from the natural over to the supernatural, you will not receive all God has for you. You will keep getting what you are getting. You will be limited by your five senses and that is not victory. You will still go to heaven but miracles and signs will not be part of your life. If you are healed of a deadly cancer by believing that by His stripes you are healed (*I Peter 2:24*), someone will take note and want to know how that is possible. You can share your testimony and show them *Isaiah 53:4* that says *"truly Jesus bore your sickness"* and that you stood on God's Word instead of what the doctor said or how you felt.

Physically we are healed in the spiritual realm but our sense of feeling says, "Sure doesn't feel like I'm healed". "I sure am not prospering. I'm three months behind on my mortgage payment".

Our minds are not being renewed to God's way of thinking. We have to change our thinking to God's way of thinking and then the physical will line up with what God says in His Word (the spiritual). The physical must submit to the spiritual. We must believe first then we will see.

This is a huge problem with Christians. Jesus said in *Luke 18:17*, *"Truly I say to you, whoever does not accept and receive and welcome the kingdom of God like a little child [does] shall not in any way enter it [at all]."* Children are gullible. They believe almost anything. We must too accept and receive the Kingdom of God like a little child. Not only receiving Him by faith as our Lord and Savior but also receiving all His promises by faith as well. We cannot see everything that He promises right now but by renewing our mind and living the way God wants us to live, we will begin to see the manifestation of what God promises us. And a reminder--the Kingdom of God is not heaven but this blessed life <u>now</u> on earth!

As you can see from the scripture from *John 4:24*, God is a Spirit. We cannot see Him with our physical eyes. Jesus Christ was God in the flesh. He walked on this earth as a man with five senses just as we have. But He is the only person who physically walked on this earth, died and took the power away from Satan and was raised again from the dead by God's power *(Ephesians 1:19-20)*. When we confess Him as our Lord and Savior, we are then a new creature *(II Corinthians 5:17)*. Everything that is true of Jesus is true of your born-again spirit *(I John 4:17)*. Our spirit's are brand new but we are still the same in our soul and body. We have the fruit of the spirit deposited in our spirit *(Galatians 5:22-23)* but that fruit has to be developed. We want to get what is in our spirit to our soul and body and we do that by renewing our mind *(Romans 12:2)*. We must get what is already inside of us (our perfect born again spirit) to the outside.

We have the fruit of the spirit deposited in our spirit, which develops our character, and we receive all the spiritual blessings in the heavenly realm. Some of those spiritual blessings God has provided are: prosperity *(II Corinthians 8:9)*, healing of our body *(Psalm 103:3 & Matthew 8:17)*, deliverance from the oppression of the devil (*Colossians 1:13 & I John 3:8*), forgiveness of our past, present and future sins (*Colossians 1:14*), and eternal life (*John 3:16 & John 17:3*).

Looking at the above blessings we receive in the spiritual realm, we see healing of our physical body. This is probably the hardest to fathom and we need to receive by faith and renew our mind to this Truth. That is the importance of the supernatural verses the natural. In the natural the doctor tells you that you have cancer and you have one year to live. But God's Word says in *Psalm 118:17 that you shall not die but live and shall declare the works and recount the illustrious acts of the Lord.* God says in *Psalm 103:3* that He forgave all your iniquities and healed **all** of your diseases. The same way He forgave your sins is the same way He healed all your diseases. <u>Who are you going to believe?</u> Are you going to believe God or the doctor? I already showed you what you receive in the spiritual realm and healing of your physical body was one of the blessings. He gives the Truth to you in *Psalms*. This is where people either do not know this Truth or look too much at the natural way of things. You must change your thinking to God's way of thinking. Otherwise you will not live in the supernatural but will live by what you feel, see, taste, smell, and hear. Most churches do not teach that healing of your physical body is one of the things Christ died for us to have. Most churches only preach the forgiveness of sins. You cannot have faith for something you are not hearing. Faith comes by hearing and hearing by the Word of God (*Romans 10:17*).

Look at it this way: When you come to Christ, you receive all the spiritual blessings from God in the heavenly realm. You receive healing of your physical body. You don't feel healed because you have arthritis. But coming to Christ you are a new creature. Look at the way God sees you and He says you are a healed person. You receive all that Jesus is and Jesus is not sick with arthritis. The devil has lied to you and stolen your inheritance that you received when you were born again. Your sickness is from the devil. People believe the devil more than they believe God. Jesus paid the price for your healing the same way He paid the price for your sins. He's already done everything. Healing is already done. We need to renew our mind and change our way of thinking and receive all that Christ has done for us.

Most Christians are trying to get God to do something He's already done over 2,000 years ago. We don't go by what our senses are telling us, we stand on the Word of God that says "by His stripes I am healed". You stand on the Word regardless of how you feel. Sometimes healing is instant and sometimes it takes time. But God always heals and God is never the problem. People will say, "I'm waiting for God to heal me." God's not the problem. There are many things that can hinder you receiving your healing and unbelief is one of them. If you don't really believe you are healed until you feel it, then unbelief is present. We must keep our eyes on Jesus and His finished work and not look at ourselves.

Maybe back pain stems from some anger you have toward someone in your past. Anger held on to will affect your physical body (*Proverbs 14:30*). It's not God who gave you back pain but envy, anger, jealousy, and bitterness can be like rottenness to the bones. Now you have work to do and must renew your mind and deal with your stuff. Renewing your mind must be constant (*Ephesians 4:23*). The church you attend doesn't teach this. Now I will not condemn any church. I pray that churches all around the world would receive this Truth. In order to take all that is yours "in Christ", you must renew your mind. Your spirit must dominate then your body and soul will line up with God's Word.

Allow the Holy Spirit to teach you all things (*John 14:26*). You will not receive all the power of God by just being water baptized. You must receive all the power that God has for you and you can receive all of His power by asking for it. You can pray the prayer to receive the baptism in the Holy Spirit at the back of this book. Tell God you want the same power that the disciples received on the day of Pentecost. Pray you receive that power with the evidence of speaking in tongues (*Acts 1:8 & 2:4*). Be determined to renew your mind and receive all that God has for you. You will never step into the supernatural realm if you keep one foot in the world and one foot in the kingdom.

What Kind Of Faith Do You Have?

I hear people often say, "I've got faith", and they are still very carnal meaning they are going by their five senses. I don't even know how to explain what they think they have. If they had real Bible faith they would be at peace. They would be at rest, which I will talk about in the next chapter. People try to have faith but don't trust God. They still look at things in the natural and maybe hope God answers their prayer. This is what faith is in the Amplified Bible:

> Now faith is the assurance (the confirmation, the title
> deed) of the things [we] hope for, being the proof of things
> [we] do not see and the conviction of their reality [faith
> perceiving as real fact what is not revealed to the senses].
> Hebrews 11:1

You can see at the end of this scripture, it says faith perceiving as real fact what is not revealed to the senses. Faith is believing in what you can't see. You can't go by your senses. Faith to me is believing what God says, period! The New King James version says that faith is the substance of things hoped for, the evidence of things not seen. If you have substance or evidence you have something concrete. Evidence is proof. If you have prayed a prayer according to the Word of God, it is evident that it will come to pass. Another word for evident is obvious. It is a sure thing that what you prayed for will manifest, but you cannot go by what you don't see. You must look into the spiritual realm. The Kingdom of God is not physical, it is spiritual. The spiritual overrules the physical, because the spiritual made the physical.

It also says, "Now faith is". Not some day, but you receive the answer to your prayer at the time you pray (Mark 11:22-24). You must renew your mind to God's Word and your faith will increase. His promises will become revelation to you. You have to continue to speak like it's already happened and you have to see what you prayed for in your imagination. There is evidence of your dream or prayer in the spiritual realm and if God put that in your heart, He will bring it to pass (*Psalm 37:4-5*). You are unable to physically see or feel what God has for you but you have to believe by faith. Use your imagination. God is not asking you to make your dreams come to pass. Do what you can do and God will do the rest. If He has you in a season of renewing your mind and trusting Him, then do that and He will give you the next step to take when it's time. He's not asking you to figure everything out--He is asking you to trust Him and He will bring your dreams to pass. That way He gets all the glory and not you. Keep renewing your mind and what is in the spiritual realm will come out in the physical realm if you don't quit. You'll have peace about the next step He asks you to take. Don't try and do something before it's time. Keep doing the last thing He told you to do and He will let you know when to take the next step.

I come across many Christians that say they have faith but there is something that always will negate their faith. "I have faith, but I won't believe it until I see it." That doesn't even make sense. If they had faith they would be standing on the end result not waiting to see what happens. They are not standing on the evidence of things not seen. There is so much of this going on. People say they have faith but not talking like it. You must speak your faith, act on it, and that boils down to speaking of the evidence and proof of the manifestation of the promises of God. You must speak the Word of God and what God says and not what you see in the natural.

I ask people that say they have faith, what they have faith for and many do not know how to answer that. They have no knowledge of the Word of God so therefore cannot speak the end result. They have no knowledge of what God promises in His Word so you can't have faith for something you don't know about.

Real faith in God is believing in the supernatural over what you see in the natural. Faith is believing what God says in His Word. We have an over and above God and we need to step into the supernatural and depart from what is usual or normal. People don't pay attention to people who are ordinary. You may get noticed but if you are extraordinary you will stand out in a crowd. Now I don't mean this in a show-off kind of way. I mean that while you are dealing with the diagnosis of cancer, you can rejoice in the Lord and declare His Word that says, "I will live and not die" (*Psalm 118:17*). You go about your everyday life as if nothing is wrong with you. You stand on the Word of God and not what the doctor says. Three months go by and you have a check-up and the doctor is puzzled because there is no trace of cancer in your body at all. That is supernatural. God gets all the glory because His Word is true.

Renew Your Mind To God's Love and Truths

You will never have this kind of faith without knowing that God loves you and without renewing your mind to God's Truth. *Galatians 5:6* says that faith works through love. How could you have faith that you are healed when you think that God doesn't love you? You have to know that God loves you and that His Son paid a huge price for your salvation, healing and prosperity. Receive all His gifts, not just a trip to heaven. Enjoy heaven on earth as God planned it. Christians are living the same as people in the world. They are getting flu shots just like their unsaved neighbor. Your flu shot should be meditating on the Word of God. *Proverbs 4:22* says that the Word of God is healing and health to all our flesh. We have to show people that we have the Holy Spirit on the inside of us-the same Holy Spirit that created heaven and earth. That's powerful.

You will never have faith for this way of living if you don't renew your mind. It is like you have to totally remove your worldly way of thinking and replace your whole brain with God's way of thinking. His way of thinking is totally opposite of what we have been taught. We will not make an impact in this world if we don't invest time in reading and studying the Word. If someone gave you a choice of $100,000 or a chance to read God's Word and have the life He had for you, I believe most would take the $100 K. They would want the immediate satisfaction and not want to invest time in finding out what God has for them. The $100 K is petty cash to a person of faith that seeks first the Kingdom of God (*Matthew 6:33*). God's way of living is far above anything we could ever do on our own. Renewing your mind to God's Word gives you Wisdom and Wisdom, according to *Proverbs 3:14*, is better than the gaining of silver and fine gold.

God told Abraham that he would be the father of many nations and he was old. Looking at his body in the natural and going by his five senses, there was no way he was able to father a child. But God spoke and Abraham believed God. *Romans 4:17* says, *"(As it is written, I have made thee a father of many nations,) before him whom he believed, even God, who quickened the dead, and calleth those things which be not as though they were." (KJV)* God called him the father of many nations and it looked impossible. If something looks impossible but God says it's possible, believe God. Believe the unbelievable! Speak it and receive it. *Second Corinthians 4:13* says, *"...We too believe, and therefore we speak."* Don't speak what you see, speak what God says even if it looks impossible. You may feel foolish. I'm sure Abraham felt foolish calling himself the father of many nations at his age. We have to walk by faith and not by what we see (*II Corinthians 5:7*). According to *Hebrews 10:36*, patience, which is cheerful endurance, is the critical force that keeps you operating in faith until you receive the promise.

God loves us so much and has such a good life for us. Find out the whole Truth for yourself. Don't believe me or some preacher on TV. Look up these scriptures and find out for yourself what God has to say. Let the Holy Spirit be your Teacher. Live the over and above, supernatural life that God has for you instead of a mediocre, natural life. Let's make God famous by showing how powerful and loving He really is.

Chapter 9

The Rest Of God Is Power

"For we which have believed do enter into <u>rest</u>,
as He said, As I have sworn in My wrath, if they
shall enter into My rest: although the works were
finished from the foundation of the world."
Hebrews 4:3 KJV

Have you ever worried about something that never even happened? Have you spent years worrying over a child or a loved one that seemed like they were going on the wrong path but eventually ended up changing? Do you worry about making ends meet? You may have been praying about things and worrying at the same time. That is not faith and you will certainly not enter the rest of God. The word <u>rest</u> means 'peace of mind or spirit.' It also means 'to cease.' My own definition is to cease from doing our own works, trust God, and receive the finished work of Jesus.

We rest because we know Jesus Christ has taken care of everything. We don't try to get God to do something but our faith is a positive response to what God has already done. When we are at rest we have <u>peace</u>. 'Peace' is freedom from disquieting or oppressive thoughts--being at ease internally and externally. The peace from Jesus is knowing that you don't have to toil and struggle to make God answer your prayers or beg God to heal you or pay your bills. He's already taken care of everything. We just have to renew our mind to what He's done, sow the Word of God in our heart, and just like a farmer puts seed in the ground, he will get what he's planted. The farmer doesn't get up in the middle of the night worrying if his seed is going to produce a harvest. He rests patiently knowing that seed will produce and eventually he'll have his harvest. We do the same thing. Rest is key in receiving all God has done for you. God's Word will always produce-<u>guaranteed</u>. We have to receive it and believe it. We must be patient and enjoy our lives while God and His angels go to work to manifest what we are believing for.

When you find out what God has for you in His Word, you will enter that supernatural rest. It is not a rest because you are tired, it is a rest knowing that God has taken care of everything for you. *Hebrews 4:3* says that God's works were finished from the foundation of the world. He's already provided healing, finances, deliverance from oppression, and forgiven your sins since the beginning. You may not see yourself healed or prosperous but it is all in the spiritual realm. **It is already done**. See yourself as God sees you. You keep doing what you need to do and God will direct your steps. God loves us unconditionally and we are redeemed from the wrath of the Old Testament. We have authority in His Word and victory in the Blood. We do not have to worry, feel guilty, or be depressed. We need to receive these Truths and they need to become revelation knowledge. What God has already done will be revealed to you and you believe everything the Word says over your five senses. We know that beyond a shadow of a doubt that by His stripes we are healed and that God always causes us to triumph. We cannot go by the way things look or go by what has happened or not happened in the past. We stand on the Word of God.

God has given us His Word to know what we have inherited and to know how to live. He has supplied us with everything we need. We have to receive all those blessings by faith. Go back to the first chapter to review what we have inherited through Christ. As I have said many times throughout this book, most Christians only believe that their sins have been forgiven and that they will go to heaven when they die. They call on God every now and then if they need some help with something. God has already supplied us with everything we need and wants us to live a blessed life beyond our highest hopes and dreams (*Ephesians 3:20*). God finished His work and didn't rest because He was tired. He rested because everything was finished. He provided everything we would ever need. Healing and prosperity have already been provided. Forgiveness of sins has been provided. Jesus doesn't have to die again so that you can be forgiven. Look at it this way. When God created the earth, He got everything ready for Adam and Eve. He had light, plants, animals, water, trees with fruit--everything they would need. Then on the sixth day He created man. He didn't create man first. He did this because He wanted to have everything ready. In the New Covenant, Jesus has already done everything for us. Salvation and all its benefits (healing, prosperity, forgiveness of sins, deliverance from every oppression) has already been provided. We need to renew our mind to these Truth's and enter into that rest knowing that everything is done. We aren't trying to get God to heal us--we receive healing by faith in the finished work of Jesus.

Christians are not resting. Most do not have peace of mind. Many are worried about their health or a loved ones health. Many are worried about finances and wondering if they will have any money when they retire. Most Christians are not living in the promises of God. People have not been taught the full Truth and have not read the Bible for themselves. They do not know all they have inherited in Christ.

Let's say you have an envelope at home that you've never opened. It doesn't look important so it just gets hidden away somewhere. Twenty years go by and you run across that envelope. You open it and you see that it is a will of someone you knew a long time ago. This will said that you had inherited ten million dollars. You would be shocked. Here you spent 20 years of your life struggling to get by when you could have had a prosperous life.

This is similar to what many Christians are doing. They have a Bible on their coffee table and never open it. It gets tossed aside or covered up with junk. People go to church and listen to a pastor that has never told them what they have in Christ. Many do not know they have to renew their mind to God's way of thinking so that they can receive everything God has for them. They have no knowledge of what to do or what they have inherited so they never enter the rest of God. They have everything they need in the Word of God but still struggle because they are either too lazy to renew their mind or just going by what their church is teaching them.

I do not know how Christians make it in this world without knowing what God has provided for them? Many do not renew their mind on a daily basis. They are basically in this world on their own and only believing they will go to heaven when they die and calling on God when they need help. People are so stubborn. They are either not wanting to give up something or they don't want to spend the time getting in the Word. Even if you tell some people that Jesus paid the price for their healing and prosperity, they don't believe it. Why would God come as a Man (Jesus) if He didn't want us to do what Jesus did? Therefore we have Christians who are acting like the people in the world. It's like the guy who was laying by the pool for 38 years (*John 5*) and Jesus asked him, *"Are you really serious about getting well?"* Jesus healed the man and then said, *"Pick up your bed and walk!"* Many people are not serious about getting well and sure don't want to do something. I want to tell people, "Pick up your Bible and renew your mind!" Realize that you don't have to be sick or broke or oppressed by depression or worry. Ask God what you need to work on and then do it. Don't just lay around feeling sorry for yourself. Get to work and renew your mind and help someone else in the mean time. "But I work a full time job. I don't have time to read the Bible." That is the biggest lie from Satan that I've ever heard. I said this before in this book. Listen to teaching CD's on your way to work. Spend time with God in the morning. Spend time with Him when you get off work. How much time do you spend watching TV? You have time. You just don't want to use it for seeking God and His Word. Get rid of that lazy, passive spirit and force yourself to spend time with God. This sounds harsh but our flesh is lazy. After awhile you will become so hungry for His Word. You will need Him more than you need physical food. Don't let the devil cheat you out of a restful, prosperous life.

I run across so many carnal Christians. A carnal Christian is someone who lives by their five senses. They can believe they are maybe forgiven of their sins and may go to heaven when they die. I say "may" because many are basing their entry in heaven on their performance. They worry, complain, and blame others or the government. They find fault with people and some spend endless time trying to get even with someone that wronged them or sue people to see what they can get out of them. It is ridiculous and a tragedy. They have not been taught the Truth. I have tried to help people like this but they tell me about the Bible. They are so stubborn and do not even hear the Truth. First of all, they are comprehending things with their mind. They are not baptized in the Holy Spirit to comprehend the Bible with their spirit. It boils down to wrong teaching, a rebellious attitude, and not knowing what has already been deposited in his or her spirit.

People believe they are going to heaven when they die but are afraid of dying. Why would anyone who truly believes they will spend eternity in heaven with Jesus be afraid of dying? A mature Christian is not afraid of dying. First of all, we have authority over sickness and disease and even if you didn't get healed you could still be joyful knowing where you are going. And we are to live heaven on earth so you won't even know you died because you've been enjoying your life on earth as it is in heaven (*Matthew 6:10*). You can't lose. Christians are not living in rest. What they've got is not revelation to them. Christians are struggling to get something they already have therefore they cannot rest.

You can see the end of *Hebrews 4:3*, it says the works were finished from the foundation of the world. I am repeating several things because it is crucial you get this. This means God has supplied everything for us since He created the earth. God had provided Adam and Eve with everything they needed. But they turned their authority over to the devil. Jesus Christ suffered in His physical body, shed His blood and took our sickness and poverty. He also took authority away from Satan. Satan is a defeated foe and has no hold on us in any way. We now have Christ living on the inside of us through the Holy Spirit and have the same power that He had when He was on this earth (*Ephesians 1:19-20*). People that do not know this are not resting.

Most of the Christians I know are not resting in the finished work of Jesus because they do not know what it all entails. People asked Jesus what are we to do that we may be working the works of God? Jesus replied by saying, "**Only believe** *in the One Whom He has sent*"*(John 6:28-29)*. The word believe means 'to put trust in and rely on God'. To put trust in and rely on God means to trust in His Word and be confident that what He says is true. The mind has to be renewed to what we have, believe it, receive revelation knowledge of the Truth and promises, and then receive them by faith.

I hear people say, "Well, I don't believe that part of the Bible." People make a big mistake when they don't believe the whole Bible. The problem is that their interpretation of the Bible may be incorrect. I am surely not 100% correct at interpreting the Bible but God says you will enter the rest of God if you believe. If you are not at rest, ask the Holy Spirit to reveal to you what you need to work on. If your prayers aren't being answered or you are restless, maybe you have unforgiveness in your heart. God says to forgive if you have anything against anyone (*Mark 11:25*). If you think there is no way you will forgive that person after what they did to you, you will not be in rest. God does not ask us to do anything that we can't do. Anything He tells us to do is for our benefit. Your life will not be powerful if you believe only parts of the Bible. You will not live a powerful life if you are not obedient to what God says to do.

This is a quote from a woman named Hannah Whitehall Smith who lived in the 1800's. She said, "Plainly the believer can do nothing but trust, while the Lord, in whom he trusts, actually does the work instructed to Him. Our part is trusting, it is His to accomplish the results." If we are trying to do God's job then we will be limited and will get human results. God can't work if we're working. It is when we rest that God can go to work.

I like the last part of that quote-our part is trusting, it is His to accomplish the results. I believe the reason it is so hard to trust God is because we want to do something ourselves. We look unto ourselves instead of unto Jesus (*Hebrews 12:1-3*). We have to know what is our part and what is God's. <u>Trusting</u> means to place confidence in or depend on. Many of us want to do things our own way. We always think we should be doing something when we should be trusting. It is also hard to trust someone you can't see. I think this is especially hard for men. Men are taught to be the bread winners. They are suppose to be the head of the household. So much pressure is put on the man. Many of them are doing things in their own strength. They are not depending on God. Most believe in God but Jesus said in *John 15:5*, *"Apart from Me, you can do nothing."* You can do things but will get human results. When you trust in God, you will get supernatural results.

I believe every negative emotion we deal with stems from not knowing God loves us, not renewing our mind to God's Word, and not trusting God. You can't really trust someone if you don't know them. If you don't know God loves you and that He has a good plan for your life, you will live in fear of many things. If you have fear about your future or finances, you do not know that God has provided your needs according to His riches in glory in Christ Jesus (*Philippians 4:19*).

Hebrews 4:3 says those who have believed do enter the rest of God. This does not only mean that those who believe in Jesus Christ will enter the rest of God. You have to know what Jesus has done for you, trust that He has already provided everything you need, receive everything by faith, and then you will be in rest. You need to do your part.

Hebrews 4:11 says we need to exert ourselves and strive diligently to enter the rest of God... Did you see that? This is not something that will just fall on you. You need to exert yourself and strive diligently to enter the rest of God. Our flesh is naturally lazy and wants to rest in a bad way, meaning laying on the couch. If you want all that God has for you, you need to get in His Word and do your part. You will be glad you did.

Rest In Him

> *"Only aim at and strive for and seek His kingdom, and*
> *all these things shall be supplied to you also. Do not be*
> *seized with alarm and struck with fear, little flock, for it*
> *is your Father's good pleasure to give you the kingdom!"*
> Luke 12:31-32

Jesus said some powerful words in the above scriptures. Notice how it says to only aim at and strive for and seek His kingdom and everything would be supplied to you. This is talking about everything you will ever need-food, clothing, protection, and much more. It does not say to strive and struggle to achieve success and purchase all kinds of high dollar items so people will think highly of you.

We need to seek God and His Kingdom. The Kingdom of God is righteousness, peace and joy in the Holy Spirit (*Romans 14:17*). *Hebrews 12:2* says to look away from all that will distract unto Jesus, the Author and Finisher of our faith (shortened). In order to enter the rest of God we must seek Jesus and Him alone. If we get focused on all the money that we need to pay our bills, we are looking at the demands on our life. We get into a "works" mentality. Look again at *Luke 12:32*. Jesus is saying to not be seized with alarm and struck with fear. It is not only God's pleasure to give us all we need but it is His **good** pleasure. God knows our needs and He will not leave us without support (*Hebrews 13:5*). He is pleased to have provided everything we need. It was all in the plan. Our Father had this arranged from the beginning. He supplied Adam and Eve with everything they needed but they turned their authority over to the devil. Jesus had to come as a Man to get that authority back. We now have everything we need and it is the Father's good pleasure to lavishly supply us with everything. We receive these blessings not because of our goodness but because of what Jesus has done. We are no longer under the Law where we have to do good to earn God's love. Thanks to Jesus Christ and the New Covenant of grace, we receive all God has for us because He loves us and we receive all Jesus deserved. Talk about

God's love for us. Look at the sacrifice Jesus made for us. Learn what your inheritance is and quit trying to meet all the demands of life by striving and struggling. Seek Jesus and only Him and you will have everything you need and more besides to help others.

Joshua received a huge responsibility after Moses died. He had to lead the people across the Jordan into the Promised Land. Those were big shoes to fill. I'm sure he was wanting to get afraid not knowing what to do. But God said to him in *Joshua 1:5, "As I was with Moses, so I will be with you; I will not fail you or forsake you."* There was no handbook that Moses left him or training on what to do. But God had all the instructions and Wisdom Joshua needed in His Word. He told Joshua in verse 8, *"This Book of the Law shall not depart out of your mouth, but you shall meditate on it day and night, that you may observe and do according to all that is written in it. For then you shall make your way prosperous, and then you shall deal wisely and have good success."*

You will be limited in what you receive from God and will not be in rest if you work hard to earn everything without renewing your mind to the Word of God. As God said to Joshua, we must meditate on the Word day and night and say what God says. Looking to Jesus and His Word is what will make you prosperous in every way and bring you good success. Get His Word in your heart. Meditate on it day and night. A businessman would be better off seeking God and His Word before he starts his day than spending time watching the stock market report or reading the newspaper.

King Solomon, who was the richest man that ever lived, said that whatever you do, seek Wisdom. He had women, riches, and anything he wanted but none of that mattered without seeking God and His Wisdom. I recommend reading all of Proverbs and take financial advice from a man who had the most money and never went bankrupt. Verse 17 of *Proverbs 3* says, *"Her ways (meaning Wisdom) are highways of pleasantness, and all her paths are peace."* Seek God and His Wisdom and you will have the path to peace and rest.

People across the world are struggling and striving to have success. Many are working themselves to the bone trying to make ends meet. In God's Word is every answer to every problem you will ever have. You will know what to do in your family life and in your business. *Proverbs 3:14* says, *"For the gaining of it (Wisdom) is better than the gaining of silver, and the profit of it better than fine gold."* When you have Wisdom, financial blessings will come. God loves us and wants us to be prosperous. There is nothing worse than just living paycheck to paycheck and barely getting by. That is not God's best for us. You may say, "But at least we're better off than most of the world." Yes, that is true. Many are homeless and do not have anything. Again, that is not God's best. The promises of God are for whosoever will. The promises of God are yes and amen in Him (*II Corinthians 1:20*). We are God's children and He wants us to be blessed and to be a blessing to others. He wants us to enjoy life and rest in Him so others will want a relationship with Jesus.

Are You Connected?

If you are reading this book, the Holy Spirit is drawing you in. God wants a relationship with you. God has such a good plan for you and He wants an intimate relationship. Maybe you are depressed and frustrated and crying out to God when you have a problem. You are stuck in a rut and can't seem to get out. You say, "I believe in Jesus. I don't know why God doesn't answer my prayers?" Or a positive unbeliever says, "just keep a good attitude, look at the positive in everything." That will only work for a small few and get you so far. Jesus and His Word are the only answer to a prosperous life. The Word of God is the only thing that can change your life. The Word of God must be sown in your heart. You must have fellowship with Him on a constant basis.

I'm going to ask you, are you connected to the vine? This is what I believe is wrong with the body of Christ (people who say they believe in Jesus Christ). Jesus said in *John 15:5*, *"I am the Vine; you are the branches. Whoever lives in Me and I in him bears much (abundant) fruit. However, apart from Me [cut off from vital union with Me] you can do nothing."*

The problem Christians have is that they are not connected to the Vine which is Jesus. They do not read His Word so that it gets into their heart. The Word of God has inherent power to change any person and any situation. God's Word is spirit and life (*John 6:63*). Our connection to God is through His Word. <u>If you are not in the Word, you are not connected to God</u>. If you are not connected to the Vine you cannot bear any fruit. If you do not read the Word and get it into your heart you will not see any results. Your life will remain the same. You will operate on human faith which is doing whatever you do and expecting God to bless it or fix it if you screwed up. *Romans 8:6* says this:

> *"Now the mind of the flesh [which is sense and*
> *reason without the Holy Spirit] is death [death that*
> *comprises all the miseries arising from sin, both here*
> *and hereafter]. But the mind of the [Holy] Spirit is*
> *life and [soul] peace [both now and forever]."*

I'm going to repeat some things and make it as simple as possible so you get it. God's Word is spirit and life (*John 6:63*). We worship God in spirit and in truth because God is a Spirit (*John 4:24*). According to *Romans 8:6* the mind of the Holy Spirit is life and peace both now and forever. The mind of the Holy Spirit, or being spiritually minded, is being Word minded. It is lining up your thinking with the Word of God. And being that God's Word is spirit and life and we worship Him in spirit and in truth then our relationship with God (because He is a Spirit) is through the Word of God. By being in the Word and seeking Jesus, because you want to know the person who wrote the Bible (*John 1:1-2*) and <u>Jesus is God</u>, (*John 1:1-4 & Colossians 1:15-17*) His Word is your connection to Him.

First John 4:1-3 says this: *"Beloved, believe not every spirit, but try the spirits whether they are of God: because many false prophets are gone out into the world. Hereby know ye the Spirit of God: <u>Every spirit that confesseth that Jesus Christ is come in the flesh is of God:</u> And every spirit that confesseth not that Jesus Christ is come in the flesh is not of God: and this is that spirit of antichrist, whereof ye have heard that it should come; and even now already is it in the world."* (*KJV*) If you don't know that Jesus Christ was God in the flesh, you are deceived. There are many religions that say that Jesus was only a prophet and he wasn't God. Other beliefs are that Jesus was a brother to Lucifer. I hear all kinds of things.

God exists in three persons-Father, Son and Holy Spirit. The Word is God Himself. Jesus came as a Man so that we could relate to Him and do what He did. Jesus understands us (*Hebrews 4:15*) because He had a physical body and a soul like we do. Jesus died so that we could have abundant life and He sent us the Holy Spirit. Jesus was a man who could only be at one place at a time. But He sent the Holy Spirit to us so that He can dwell in every believer (*John 16:7*). If *Romans 8:6* says that the mind of the Holy Spirit is life and peace both now and forever then we are to have life and peace right now where we are at. Some people think they won't have peace until they get to heaven. We are to have peace now. But the only way we will have peace is by being connected to the Vine, being in the Word, and lining up our thinking with God's Word. No Word, no connection to Jesus, no life and peace.

You say, "I'm not in the Word but I believe in Jesus. Does that mean I won't go to heaven?" At one point, you were connected by His Word. You heard preaching about Jesus and then said a prayer that you believed in your heart (*Romans 10:9-10*). You will go to heaven if you believe in Jesus Christ, but to receive all God has for you here on earth, you need to be connected. To have the peace that passes all understanding, you need to learn God's ways through His word.

So if you know that something is missing or you say, "I know there is more to life", then the something you are missing is actually a Person and His Name is Jesus. Even if you say you believe in Him but your life is not full of life and peace, then you need to get honest with yourself and get connected to the Vine. Get into the Word and let the Word of God clean you up. Renew you mind to the Word of God so that you may prove for yourselves what is the perfect will of God (*Romans 12:2*).

There are some of you that are doing this. You are connected to Jesus and you spend time with Him and His Word every day. You know this is the answer for everyone yet you are frustrated over someone in your family or workplace that is such a mess. You have shared Jesus with them and recommended them getting into the Word. You have spent time sharing scriptures with them and even so much as typing the scriptures out for them. You have given them CD's and DVD's of people to listen to that preach the Word of Faith and nothing seems to change in their life because they haven't made any attempt to read or listen to anything. That person at work or that family member says they believe in Jesus and they seem to listen to you but they continue to be a mess because they are not renewing their mind. My advice to you is **let it go**. The Holy Spirit is dealing with them and He is the only one that can draw them in. You can love them and encourage them to get in the Word but if they don't, you've done as much as you can. Continue to be a peaceful person and people will see the fruit in your life. Ask the Lord to show you how to love that person and encourage them. It is the goodness of God that leads men to repentance (*Romans 2:4*). Eventually they will get a clue and think, "Maybe I should get in the Word".

The only way to recognize a spiritually mature person is when nothing bothers them. They are not bothered by their circumstances. They are always peaceful and joyful no matter what because of Who they know. Their house could burn down with their hair on fire and they would say, "I'm trusting God because He always causes me to triumph. He supplies all of my needs and knows what I need. I'll have even a better and bigger house and my hair will grow back thicker and more beautiful. So in the meantime I know God will supply a wig for me to wear". The spiritually mature person knows who their Daddy (Father God) is and walks in victory no matter what. They rest in the finished work of Jesus and become a huge witness for Christ.

Connected, Rested And Powerful Or Disconnected, Tired And Powerless?

As I bring this book to a close, I want to point out the main things we need to do to be a witness for Christ on the earth in these final days. Why would anyone not want to have all Jesus Christ died for them to have? You have a chance now to renew your mind to the

Word of God and receive all He has for you. This will take discipline and work but it will be worth it. Don't just think of yourself--think of how your life will change and think of all the people that can be helped by you being obedient to the Word of God. Today many people are very rebellious. The word 'rebellious' means opposing or defying authority. People don't want to be under any type of authority. We see that in people of all ages today. Many young people don't have parents that are disciplining them. Most come from broken homes and have never been disciplined. They have not grown up being taught the Word of God. What is the answer? Showing people the real love of Jesus instead of religious rules and hypocritical attitudes. There are so many religions that are based on performance and people see this and have experienced religion and then have a bad taste in their mouth about Christianity. We need to love the unlovely and find out how to be a witness for Christ so we can win people over and show them what it is really like to be a Christian.

Ezekiel 12:2 says this: *"Son of man, you dwell in the midst of the house of the rebellious, who have eyes to see and see not, who have ears to hear and hear not, for they are a rebellious house."* People are rebellious and resisting God because they see Him as a mean and critical god. They haven't heard the Truth preached and demonstrated. We need to preach Jesus and show them unconditional love that God shows us. People need to know Jesus and receive the baptism in the Holy Spirit and renew their mind to the Word of God.

You need spiritual ears and eyes to understand the Word of God. Jesus said in the end of *Mark 8*, *"Are your hearts in [a settled state of] hardness?"* They were more in tune to what they could see than to the supernatural realm. They had seen the miracle of the multiplying of the loaves and fishes and still went back to seeing things in the natural realm. They had not yet received the Holy Spirit and were seeing with their natural eyes and mind. We must also receive the baptism in the Holy Spirit to understand these Truths. You need spiritual ears and eyes to understand the Word.

The rebellious group Ezekiel is talking about in the above scripture is people who hear the Word but don't listen. How can they listen without the Spirit of God in them--they only comprehend with their mind and you cannot understand the Word of God without the Spirit of God. *Ezekiel 11:19* says God will give them a new heart that is responsive to the touch of their God. The Holy Spirit will control you, draw you in. The Holy Spirit is your interpreter. He will reveal the Word to you. I feel like I'm talking a foreign language when I talk faith. It is because the people are trying to understand with their minds. They are not baptized in the Holy Spirit. Therefore they are unable to receive what the Word of God has for them--they are rebellious, closed minded, and living by their five senses. We have a majority of carnal Christians living like the people in the world.

As long as Christians are living by their five senses, their will be minimal fruit in their lives. We must walk in the Spirit then we will not fulfill the lusts of the flesh (*Galatians 5:16*). Walking in the Spirit is walking by the Word of God. Our spirit is designed to believe what it doesn't see. Our spirit believes the Word of God but our mind believes what it can see. Without the baptism in the Holy Spirit, people will only comprehend the Word of God with their natural mind and that won't work. We need the baptism in the Holy Spirit to understand the Word. Jesus said in *Luke 8:11* that the seed is the Word of God. The Word of God has to be sown in our hearts. We need to renew our minds on a daily basis if we are going to be victorious. We have to exchange our thoughts for God's thoughts and say what God says. The Word of God sown in your heart is the only thing that will change you. You must receive the baptism in the Holy Spirit to be able to understand the Word. You must be determined to want to change.

Deuteronomy 30:14 says, "*But the word is very near you, in your mouth and in your mind and in your heart, so that you can do it.*" You have to renew your mind to the Word of God because the Word is your only connection to the spiritual realm. The Word of God has the inherent power to do what it says. I speak faith to many carnal Christians and they agree but then speak doubt and unbelief. It is so frustrating. I can talk to a carnal Christian who just lost their job and they will tell me all about it and say that they hope they find another job. I don't care if it's not full time, etc. I'll say, "Don't say you won't receive full-time. God will give you the desires of your heart. Believe you receive that job that is over and above of what you had before and rest. God will supply your needs and He directs your steps. He wants you to prosper. Believe Him for a better job and thank Him in advance for it." I tell them to confess out loud "Thank You, Father for that job at _____" (you fill in the blank). They just don't get it and go back to saying what they said earlier. They only comprehend things with their senses and therefore are stuck in limbo. Those kind of Christians are everywhere and people have to wake up and get a clue. You have to ask yourself if you are satisfied with your life? Are you affecting someone else's life? Are you healed and prosperous in every area? If not, quit going around the same mountain and do what I say in this book. This is what Christ wanted. These are not my instructions, these are the instruction of Jesus.

We have four types of Christians--the religious group who are living in the Old Testament and have to follow a bunch of rules, the others who are living in the Old and New Testament, Christians that are hearing a watered down version of the Gospel, and then a small group who are believing the Full Gospel and seeing people healed and delivered in every way. The time has come for the last group to stick out and affect others.

Your relationship with God is a journey and is so rewarding. You will not get saved and baptized in the Holy Spirit and have everything be perfect. God will change you. Work with Him to become all that He wants you to be. Patience is key in this journey. *Hebrews 6:12* says this:

> *"In order that you may not grow disinterested and become [spiritual] sluggards, but imitators, behaving as do those who through faith (by their leaning of the entire personality on God in Christ in absolute trust and confidence in His power, wisdom, and goodness) and by practice of patient endurance and waiting are [now] inheriting the promises.*

The promises of God come through faith and patience. Patience is a fruit of the spirit and must be developed. As you renew your mind to the Word of God and live life connected to Jesus, you will see promises fulfilled. Not everything will go smooth. If anything, as a Christian, you will go through trials and tribulation. You will suffer persecution because of the Word (*Mark 4:17*). But as Jesus said in *John 16:33*, cheer up for He has overcome the world. God is your Daddy and will help you and you are victorious already.

When you are in rest, you will have power to overcome anything that comes against you. When you rest, God can work. If you are trying to fix your problem, God is saying, "You think you can take care of this? Let's see how that works out." Patience and faith are powerful forces. Faith is trusting in God, trusting in His promises and what you can't see. Patience is the ability to persevere calmly when faced with difficulties. Patience has the power to endure whatever comes with good temper. Release your faith, develop patience, and you will inherit all God has for you. You believe and God does all the work. How awesome is that? Of course, this is not a lazy thing where you just sit back and do nothing. You do your part and God will do His.

Rest in the finished work of Jesus. Renew your mind to His Truth and trust Him. Trusting in what you can't see is not easy but that's why our God is supernatural. He is looking for people who will do their part and believe Him. The people of the Old Testament did not have the indwelling presence of the Holy Spirit. He came upon them at times. Now, as believers in Jesus Christ, He dwells in us. When Jesus said we can do greater works (*John 14:12*), He is actually saying we can do greater works than Abraham, Moses, Joshua, David, and Daniel, just to name a few. Jesus said we can do greater works than Him. But let's start by doing what He did before we get caught up in thinking we can do greater works. Be bold and pray for the sick, see blind eyes open and the dead raised. This is when people will start to believe the Gospel. This is when people will believe on the Lord Jesus Christ as their Lord and Savior. We have to have a relationship with God. He is our only answer. He created us and has such a huge plan for us. Quit working 16 hour days to make a living. Get to know your Heavenly Father and learn His way of being and doing things. King Solomon, who had everything, finally figured it out in the end, said this in *Ecclesiastes 12:13*:

> *"All has been heard; the end of the matter is: Fear*
> *God [revere and worship Him, knowing that He is]*
> *and keep His commandments, for this is the whole*
> *of man [the full, original purpose of his creation, the*
> *object of God's providence, the root of character, the*
> *foundation of all happiness, the adjustment to all*
> *inharmonious circumstances and conditions under*
> *the sun] and the whole [duty] for every man."*

Rest in the finished work of Jesus. Renew your mind to His Word and speak His Truth over what you see, feel, and hear. God wants you to have a blessed life. He wants you to live the "good life". You are His child and if you are a child then you have an inheritance from your Heavenly Father (*Romans 8:16-17*). But don't keep this to yourself. Tell everyone about Jesus. The best way to do this is to preach Jesus to everyone and when necessary, use words. Don't be a religious phony. Show His love to the world. People want to know that they are loved. You may be their only connection to God.

Be bold and pray for people at work, in school, in the market place, and wherever you see a need. Find out what you have inherited and begin to walk in your authority. Come to know Jesus and His way and then others will want what you have. Rest in His finished work. People will notice there is something different about you and that will give you an opportunity to share Jesus with them. There will be a domino effect and more and more will come to know the One and Only Way to Heaven, Jesus Christ. But remember, we don't wait to live the "good life" until after we die. When you have a relationship with Jesus Christ, Heaven starts the day you come to Him. Start Heaven on earth today!

> *"Come to Me, all you who labor and are heavy-laden*
> *and overburdened, and I will cause you to rest. [I*
> *will ease and relieve and refresh your souls.]"*
> *Matthew 11:28*

To Receive Jesus As Your Savior And Receive The Baptism in the Holy Spirit

To make Jesus your Lord and Savior, pray this prayer:

Romans 10:9 *"Because if you acknowledge and confess with your lips that Jesus is Lord and in your heart believe (adhere to, trust in, and rely on the truth) that God raised Him from the dead, you will be saved."*

Heavenly Father, I come to you in the Name of Jesus. I make Jesus the Lord of my life and I believe that You raised Him from the dead and He now lives in me. I know now that I am saved and not only will spend eternity with You in heaven but will receive all Your blessings now to fulfill the call You have on my life. Thank You for loving me and forgiving me of all my sins, past, present and future. Amen

To receive the Baptism in the Holy Spirit:

Luke 11:13 *"If you then, evil as you are, know how to give good gifts [gifts that are to their advantage] to your children, how much more will your heavenly Father give the Holy Spirit to those who ask and continue to ask Him!"*

Father God, I am asking you to baptize me with the Holy Spirit so that I may receive all the power that You have for me. Give me the same power that the disciples received on the day of Pentecost and give me the gift of speaking in tongues. By faith, I receive Your full power and the gift of tongues. Thank You, Holy Spirit for making Your home in me. Amen. (Open your mouth in faith and begin to speak in other tongues.)

You are now born again. Your spirit is brand new and God sees you just as He sees Jesus. You have the same power that raised Christ from the dead (*Ephesians 1:19-20*). You are still the same on the outside but the only way for your outside to line up with your spirit (what's inside) is to renew your mind to God's Word (*Romans 12:1-2*). Study the scriptures throughout this book and confess God's word out loud. Pray in tongues. Get into a church that teaches the Full Gospel. You are on your journey of your new life in Christ. You have received every blessing you need to do God's will on this earth (*Ephesians 1:3*). Renew your mind, bask in the Father's love for you, love God and love people. Enjoy heaven on earth-do not wait until heaven to enjoy all God has for you. Renew your mind and find out all the abundance that God has for you so you can share His wealth and Truth with others. Welcome to the family!

Romans 10:9-10 Because if you acknowledge and confess with your lips that Jesus is Lord and in your heart believe (adhere to, trust in, and rely on the truth) that God raised Him from the dead, you will be saved. For with the heart a person believes (adheres to, trusts in, and relies on Christ) and so is justified (declared righteous, acceptable to God), and with the mouth he confesses (declares openly and speaks out freely his faith) and confirms [his] salvation.

Acts 2:4 And they were all filled (diffused throughout their souls) with the Holy Spirit and began to speak in other (different, foreign) languages (tongues), as the Spirit kept giving them clear and loud expression [in each tongue in appropriate words].

Matthew 10:7-8 And as you go, preach, saying, The kingdom of heaven is at hand! Cure the sick, raise the dead, cleanse the lepers, drive out demons. Freely (without pay) you have received, freely (without charge) give.

Mark 16:17-18 And these attesting signs will accompany those who believe: in My name they will drive out demons; they will speak in new languages; They will pick up serpents; and [even] if they drink anything deadly, it will not hurt them; they will lay their hands on the sick, and they will get well.

II Corinthians 5:17 Therefore if any person is [ingrafted] in Christ (the Messiah) he is a new creation (a new creature altogether); the old [previous moral and spiritual condition] has passed away. Behold, the fresh and new has come!

Scriptures To
Renew Your Mind

Renew your mind to these truths and confess them out loud

John 10:10 The thief comes only in order to steal and kill and destroy. I came that they may have and enjoy life, and have it in abundance (to the full, till it overflows).

John 16:33 (shortened) In the world you have tribulations and trials and distress and frustration; but be of good cheer [take courage; be confident, certain, undaunted]! For I have overcome the world. [I have deprived it of power to harm you and have conquered it for you.]

Deuteronomy 8:18 But you shall [earnestly] remember the Lord your God, for it is He Who gives you power to get wealth, that He may establish His covenant which He swore to your fathers, as it is this day.

Psalm 111:5 He has given food and provision to those who reverently and worshipfully fear Him; He will remember His covenant forever and imprint it [on His mind].

Proverbs 10:22 The blessing of the Lord-it makes [truly] rich, and He adds no sorrow with it [neither does toiling increase it].

Isaiah 48:17 Thus says the Lord, your Redeemer, the Holy One of Israel: I am the Lord your God, Who teaches you to profit, Who leads you in the way that you should go.

Malachi 3:10-11 Bring all the tithes (the whole tenth of your income) into the storehouse, that there may be food in My house, and prove Me now by it, says the Lord of hosts, if I will not open the windows of heaven for you and pour you out a blessing, that there shall not be room enough to receive it. And I will rebuke the devourer [insects and plagues] for your sakes and he shall not destroy the fruits of your ground, neither shall your vine drop its fruit before the time in the field, says the Lord of hosts.

Luke 6:38 Give and [gifts] will be given to you; good measure, pressed down, shaken together, and running over, will they pour into [the pouch formed by] the bosom [of your robe and used as a bag]. For with the measure you deal out [with the measure you use when you confer benefits on others], it will be measured back to you.

Romans 13:8 Keep out of debt and owe no man anything, except to love one another...

Philippians 4:19 And my God will liberally supply [fill to the full] your every need according to His riches in glory in Christ Jesus.

III John 2 Beloved, I pray that you may prosper in every way and [that your body] may keep well, even as [I know] your soul keeps well and prospers.

*Psalm 103:2-3 Bless the Lord, O my soul, and forget not all His benefits-- Who forgives all your iniquities, **Who heals all your diseases**.*

Psalm 107:20 He sends forth His Word and heals them and rescues them from the pit and destruction.

Psalm 118:17 I shall not die but live, and shall declare the works and recount the illustrious acts of the Lord.

Psalm 91:10 There shall no evil befall you, nor any plague or calamity come near your tent.

Proverbs 4:20-23 My son, attend to My Words; consent and submit to My sayings. Let them (words) not depart from your sight; keep them (words) in the center of your heart. For they (words) are life to those who find them, <u>healing and health to all their flesh</u>.

Proverbs 3:5-8 Lean on, trust in, and be confident in the Lord with all your heart and mind and do not rely on your own insight or understanding. In all your ways know, recognize and acknowledge Him, and He will direct and make straight and plain your paths. Be not wise in your own eyes; reverently fear and worship the Lord and turn [entirely] away from evil. <u>It shall be health to your nerves and sinews, and marrow and moistening to your bones.</u>

Proverbs 17:22 A happy heart is good medicine and a cheerful mind works healing, but a broken spirit (worried spirit) dries up the bones.

*Isaiah 53:4-5 Surely He has borne our griefs (sicknesses, weaknesses, and distresses) and carried our sorrows and pains [of punishment], yet we [ignorantly] considered Him stricken, smitten and afflicted by God [as if with leprosy]. But He was wounded for our transgressions, He was bruised for our guilt and iniquities; the chastisement [needful to obtain] peace and well-being for us was upon Him, **<u>and with the stripes [that wounded] Him we are healed and made whole.</u>***

Jeremiah 30:17 For I will restore health to you and I will heal your wounds, says the Lord...

I Peter 2:24 He (Jesus) personally bore our sins in His [own] body on the tree [as on an altar and offered Himself on it], that we might die (cease to exist) to sin and live to righteousness. **_By His wounds you have been healed_**.

Matthew 8:17 And thus He fulfilled what was spoken by the prophet Isaiah, He Himself took [in order to carry away] our weaknesses and infirmities and bore away our diseases.

Psalm 54:7 For He has delivered me out of every trouble, and my eye has looked [in triumph] on my enemies.

II Corinthians 2:14 But thanks be to God, Who in Christ always leads us in triumph [as trophies of Christ's victory] and through us spreads and makes evident the fragrance of the knowledge of God everywhere.